# THE
# HEART-POWERED
## PATH

*99 Daily Practices for*
*Igniting Heart/Mind Coherence*

# ED CONRAD

LUMINARE PRESS
WWW.LUMINAREPRESS.COM

THE HEART-POWERED PATH
99 Daily Practices for Igniting Heart/Mind Coherence
www.heartpoweredpath.com
© 2018 Ed Conrad

Printed in the United States of America

Cover Design: Claire Flint Last

Luminare Press
438 Charnelton St., Suite 101
Eugene, OR 97401
www.luminarepress.com

LCCN: 2018941925
ISBN: 978-1-944733-75-9

*To all my brothers in the Mankind Project:*
*Your courage, vulnerability, and love*
*have been a shining light.*

# Gratitudes

Thank you Candyce for sharing your heart of wisdom and for the many hours of editing time and expertise you contributed to the creation of this handbook. And, I am so grateful for your constant encouragement and love. I love you.

This tool for igniting heart/mind coherence is an experiential guide for those yearning for a deeper relationship with the sacred heart of the human experience. The inspiration for this creation is a wide stream of heart-wisdom which I have been fortunate to experience over the past forty-five years. Deep appreciation goes out to the following wayshowers: Kahlil Gibran, Gregg Braden, Brene Brown, Bill Baker, Lance Secretan, The HeartMath Institute, Wayne Muller, Michael Singer, Anita Moorjani, Mark Nepo, Deepak Chopra, Dr. Paul Pearsall, Rev. Sallye Taylor, Neil Douglas-Klotz, Mahatma Gandhi, Dr. Martin Luther King, Jr., Bishop John Shelby Spong, Terri Tempest Williams, Martha Beck, Michael Meade, John Rudiger, Joyce Strahn, Dennis Chandler, Samuel Baseler, and Marsha McCool.

To all the shining lights who have showed up in my life and loved me and listened to me and led me and pushed me to heal and open my heart, from Bozeman, to Unity Village, to Savannah, to Hilton Head Island, to Denver, to Boulder, to Grand Junction, to Eau Claire, to Minneapolis and St. Paul, to Fort Worth, to Eugene, I reach out to you in gratitude for your gifts of love.

And, from my heart, I give thanks for my family; Mom and Dad- Pat and Earl Conrad, my grandparents Doc, Connie, and Belle, my sisters Julie Taylor and Diane Palladino, my daughter Hillary Lampers and my son Zachary Conrad, and my five grandchildren: Elise, Pailey, Corah, Tanna, and Max. I love you all...always.

# Introduction

We are connected. Our shared human bond is everlasting. All the noise within and without doesn't alter or discount this truth. Experiencing our deep connection with each other and our bond with life in all its forms are the foundation of who we are and why we have taken birth.

Love is the center and forms the circumference of this interconnectedness. This ground of being is everywhere present. *The Heart-Powered Path* reclaims our bond and heals our shadows of separation by synchronizing the powers of the heart with the gifts of the mind.

In order to bring about this natural partnership, it is paramount to develop the ability to craft a direct and clear connection with the heart. Because the apparatus of the thinking mind has become so tightly entwined in how we consciously process our lives, our world, and our identity, consistent practice of being heart-connected and heart-empowered has become a must in order to restore ourselves to our rightful balance and true nature.

We are in need of a new navigation system for living in a world of rapid change and information overload. Based on my own extensive experience and research and the latest scientific findings, this navigation system is a consciousness infused with the energetic frequency and emotional intelligence of the powerful heart in coherence with the brain. This evolution in consciousness makes it far less likely that one could be overpowered by the brain and nervous system's reactive and conditioned patterns. Instead, it leads to higher brain function and more balanced emotional processing.

This handbook of heart-powered practices clearly aims to shift your attention from your conditioned mind and the neurotic voice in your head, to the unconditioned, transformational capacities of the heart in coherence with the brain/mind. This long awaited and swiftly approaching shift in how to be powerful, compassionate, wise, and balanced in today's world is upon us. The challenge is significant.

Originally published in November 2014, the revised, updated version of *Heart Power: Going Deeper Into the Heart of Who You Are* was published in May of 2018. Composed of 366 reflections on the uncharted wilderness of my heart, this daily reader was a full-fledged leap into facing and making sense of the scattered pieces of my life experience.

The following is an edited excerpt from my writing for March 18, my birthday: "There are moments of truth in everyone's life that invite us to lean into something even if it terrifies us. So, I'm leaning. I'm leaning into the depth and breadth of my heart…all of it.

Yes, it is an extraordinary electromechanical pump. Also, we are familiar with the perception and portrayal of the heart as the storehouse of painful memories and sweet sentiments.

I have been compelled for a very long time to look deeper. Those of us who do, join with others over past millennia who have done the same. We are scientists, mystics, musicians, lovers, artists, philosophers, writers, healers, and inspirational leaders. Through my own exploration, I have come to know that the heart is a resilient presence in each one of us which sources and manifests life's beautiful possibilities even when the whole world may seem to be collapsing into an abyss.

This divinely human capacity is outrageously awe-inspiring. As the years have passed, I have found myself staring more and more into the marrow of my own life and longing to access and put into practice this kind of heart-powered resourcefulness."

Frequently in this handbook, you will be asked to bring your full attention to your heart or "heartspace." Each time you do, scientific research confirms there are three simple steps you can take to create balancing, healing, and inspiring effects:

⁎ *First, physically touch your heartspace with your hand in that indentation near your sternum. This can be done in various ways: one or several fingers, an open palm, hands crossed with thumbs touching or a prayer mudra with palms together. This always draws your focus away from the mind and to the heart and signals that you are turning inward.*

⁎ *Second, while keeping your awareness centered in your heart, breathe slowly and deeply allowing at least 5-7 seconds for each inhale and each exhale. With each breath, it is as if you are breathing in and breathing out through your heart. Stress hormones will subside and most importantly, this slow, deep breathing sends a message to the brain that you are safe.*

⁎ *Third, hold a quality of feeling in your heartspace. The following five feelings create a coherent synergy with the brain: gratitude, appreciation, care, compassion, or wonder. Choose one of these and bring that feeling into your heart. It may be helpful to recall an experience in which you actually felt one of these feelings. Stay with this feeling coupled with your heart and breath connection for 1-2 minutes.*

Most of the heart-powered practices include the suggestion to connect with your heartspace. Use those three simple steps as a method for creating this connection.

These 99 heart-powered practices aren't a one-time fix for what ails you. However, when integrated into daily life over time, you very well may experience in varying numbers and degrees, but not limited to, the following twelve shifts:

1. Increased intuitive and cognitive capacity
2. Greater access to the positive power of emotion
3. Living more authentically and aligned with your true purpose
4. Quieting of the fearful, judgmental voice inside your head
5. Greater capacity to connect with and inspire others
6. A healing, breakthrough effect
7. A deeper connection with the love and compassion inside of you
8. Improved ability to stay open and not shut down emotionally
9. Greater aliveness and understanding of the science of energy
10. Growth in courage and resilience
11. Enhanced creativity
12. A spiritual awakening

Almost all of these writings have a preface to the practice itself. Each practice is highlighted in italics. Some are simple. Some are progressive with several steps.

The most important aspect of this experience is to integrate these practices into your daily life. They could be followed in the order presented or in any order. There will be certain practices you will be drawn to more than others. Use this resource according to your guidance. Certain practice themes repeat. This repetition helps to integrate the changes needed to establish new empowering patterns in heart rhythms, consciousness, and emotional processing. This handbook is a primer for awakening your heart and its power in your life.

*"The heart generates all of the earthly emotions*

*as well as the blissful emotions of the higher realms.*

*But it is so much more than just emotion.*

*It is infinite awareness, and the basis of*

*all the higher consciousness you will ever assimilate.*

*It is from this power, within the center of your being,*

*that the entire script of your life is written.*

*Live in your heart—not in your mind—*

*to fulfill the script of your life or to rewrite it.*

*Your mind is powerless to bring that about.*

*But every desire of your heart will be fulfilled."*

—Glenda Green
*Love Without End: Jesus Speaks*

*Ed Conrad*

PRACTICE #1

# Return of Presence

*"The goal of life is to make your heartbeat match the beat of the universe..."*
—Joseph Campbell—

It is challenging for overdoers to remain open and present and let the urgency to be doing something flow on by. Doing becomes a preoccupation. Having the presence of heart and mind to create a healthy balance of doing and being is elusive.

Balance comes when, as a matter of course, you take to heart the mantra of radical self-care and include in the rhythm of everyday life essential interludes of presence. They can be bite-size.

This simple routine will move you toward your natural balance point. It's time to begin.

*Periodically throughout your day, stop and take a leave-of-absence from mentally processing or physically doing.*

*Have at least three bite-size moments of emptying, about two minutes each. Become still and quiet. Breathe slowly and effortlessly with your conscious attention only on your heart and the space around it. That's it.*

*There is no task to do, no place to go, no problem to solve.*

# Forgiving Yourself

*"The practice of forgiveness is our most important
contribution to the healing of the world."*

—Marianne Williamson—

If you are waiting for someone to forgive you and release you from your feelings of shame or guilt for something you have done, forgiveness and release may never come. Along the same lines, if you were truly harmed and aren't willing to forgive the perpetrator until they come to you and admit their shame and sorrow, your chance to forgive and heal your pain will likely pass you by.

All forms of forgiveness take place because you choose to end the domination of the angry, hurt, guilt-ridden voice within you. You do whatever it takes to be free and whole again. No one can do this for you. You may need allies and encouragement, but ultimately it is a conscious, courageous choice only you can make.

* *Become still. Breathe slowly and fully into the space in and around your heart. Stay with this heart connection for a minute or two.*

* *Bring into your awareness a person who hasn't forgiven you or, vice-versa, you haven't forgiven. Allow any feelings to arise.*

* *In this present moment, choose what you truly want for yourself: the growing emotional toll of harboring unforgiveness, guilt, injustice or something else, such as peace or freedom.*

* *Gently bring this phrase into your heartspace: "Sovereign Spirit of Peace and Healing within me, untie these knots of unforgiveness and set me free." Repeat as often as you choose.*

* *Know and receive into your whole being that it is this Sovereign Spirit in you that unties your knots of shame, anger, resentment, injustice, and guilt. Choose to let this Spirit moving through you have Its way.*

PRACTICE #3

# Eye Contact

*"We've become so focused on that tiny screen that we forget the big picture, the people right in front of us."*
—Regina Brett—

Making eye contact is powerful medicine especially when you find yourself in anxious moments with another or in moments that you want to truly connect with someone who is troubled. It communicates that the human being in you sees and feels the human being in them. It truly helps to ease any sense of separation or threat.

Eye contact brings to life the well-known saying that the eyes are the windows to the soul. Take this to heart.

* *Exercise the power of initiating eye contact throughout your day. Whether you are wanting to transform a stressful moment with someone or simply wanting to truly connect, initiate eye contact. Notice what you feel.*

* *While making eye contact feel and breathe into your heart. This deepens your connection even more. Magical shifts occur.*

# Remembrance

*"I am large. I contain multitudes."*
—Walt Whitman, *"Song of Myself"*—

Remembrance is the gift of reconnecting with what you already know. It is like looking into the night sky in the same direction as last week and seeing a grand constellation which the turning of time reveals, a constellation forgotten but now remembered.

What do you know in your heart-of-hearts and yet forget? Who would you be if you lived in remembrance of who and what you truly are rather than being lost in forgetfulness?

This heart-powered practice is an invitation to proactively choose to stand for your vast, limitless spirit.

*It begins with this question: "What becomes possible for me if the fearful voice inside my head is silenced?" Centered in your heart, reflect on this question for several minutes.*

*Make note of what arises in your conscious awareness.*

*Now imagine a vista: the top of a hill, an upper floor window or balcony, or whatever vista you can envision. Wherever it is, allow this expansive viewpoint to arouse in your imagination the grand nature of the universe and you. Remember you are a child of the universe.*

*May this remembrance which arises from deep inside of you remain in your inner vision. From your heart, commit to stay attuned to this expanse today.*

# Restoration of Light

*"There is in all visible things...a hidden wholeness."*
—Thomas Merton—

You came into this world tender as a blossom. You opened to the life before you. You adapted to whatever came your way even when it was painful and distorted. Underneath it all was an essence untouched by the world's lies.

At this stage of your life, it's a matter of your heart assisting you in peeling away the distortions and revealing the treasure in you, the very same unconditioned you who came into this world as a light for all to see and cherish.

* *Dedicate some time today and ask the radiant light of your soul to be switched on in your conscious awareness. Do this as you place your attention in your heart.*

* *Ask this light to pour into all of you, every single nook and cranny of your being, even the dark and gloomy places. Feel this healing and restoration coming over you now. On this day, be the central sun in your life and in the life of others.*

# Unstructured Time

*"There are always a million reasons to keep going,*
*but never a good reason to stop."*

—Wayne Muller—

A woman I know goes to extra lengths to make sure her daughter has unstructured time for play and creative exploration. The irony is that this mother conserves little or no unstructured time for her soul and spirit. She's not only bothered by it, she's feeling the life force being drained out of her. Little is left for her well-being. Like many others I have known, this imbalance becomes so ingrained, she struggles to act on her own behalf.

    *Unstructured time and space to explore, create, breathe and relax into the moment is native to who we are. Reclaim it. Put it on your daily schedule.*

    *Renew your love for your whole life. It's essential. Who would you become if you created unstructured time for yourself daily?*

PRACTICE #7

# Be the Prayer

*"For what is prayer but the expansion of yourself into the living ether."*
—Kahlil Gibran, *The Prophet*—

Prayer is not an intervention as much as it is communion, a deep feeling, an inner creative exploration guided by the feelings and visions of the heart.

Reimagine prayer. Rather than pray for love to come into your life, *be* love. In other words, be and feel what you are asking for.

* *Go to a quiet place and begin.*

* *Use your power of creation and generate the feeling of love which can be activated through your heart and your senses.*

* *In your inner hearing, hear the sound of a lover's tender voice. In your inner sense of touch, feel the gentle energy from the loving hands of someone you cherish. With your inner sight and hearing, view the sight and hear the sounds of a memorable landscape and the feelings of wonder it inspires in you. Hear the sound and feel the vibration of beautiful music.*

* *Let these expansive, evocative feelings fill you up to overflowing for several minutes. You are now literally becoming the prayer.*

* *In your fullness, feel gratitude for this energy treatment of love and inspiration you are creating.*

* *Then, if you choose, place any concern or need you may have into this frequency of love and allow it to be completely embraced by the power and tenderness of this energy.*

# A One and Only

*"This is my prayer...cherish the day."*

—Sade—

Many first time experiences of a beautiful place or a lovely soul or a chance meeting may very well be the only time. If you know in advance that an experience is likely to be a one and only, you are likely to be much more open, bold, and curious.

You know this is it. There will be no second opportunity to improve upon the first time. Tendencies toward apathy fade. You seize the moment and wake up to the rare and precious value of what is about to happen.

It is often the case that you don't know whether what is about to happen is going to be the only time you will have that unique experience. May this day become filled with the scent of a one and only.

* *Recall a time when you had a beautiful experience, a one and only, and how you cherished it. You likely still do. For several moments, resonate with the feelings of deep appreciation which went with it.*

* *Light the flame and feel the warmth of these powerful feelings of deep appreciation and let them resonate within your heart throughout your day. Choose to open this day and become filled with the energy and anticipation of a one and only. Serendipity will likely show up.*

PRACTICE #9

# Connecting with Life's Thread

*"There's a thread you follow...it is hard for others to see...*
*While you hold it you can't get lost. You don't ever let go of the thread."*
—William Stafford—

This thread of your one-of-a-kind life experience is pulling you gently forward.

* *Close your eyes and bring your full attention to the area around your heart. Imagine you are breathing in and out through your heart.*

* *Now, gently connect with the thread of your meandering path of your time on earth, you and only you making your way through all your experiences. Only you know what you've been through and all that you have felt and chosen to do. Acknowledge and give thanks for your resilience.*

* *Feel this thread of life gently tugging at you. It is very strong and pliable. This safe connection invites you to relax, let go, and trust. You are well-cared-for. This has always been the case. This is true right now.*

* *Centered in your heartspace, take a few more moments to be still and breathe effortlessly while the energy moving through you strengthens your connection with your life's thread.*

* *When you're ready, slowly open your eyes. Remain in the awareness of this life-sustaining presence enfolding you throughout your day like a melody composed just for you.*

PRACTICE #10

# Failing Upward

*"Failure is an opportunity."*

—Lao-Tzu, from the *Tao te Ching*—

In the Taoist tradition, a failure is understood as one step of an upward climb which places you closer to the full realization of happiness and fulfillment.

Your feeling of failure is often a failure of courage. You choose to allow fear or conformity to chip away at your integrity and resolve. Failures of courage stir bitterness and judgment around and around in your mind and body creating a toxic effect.

Or, you take notice of the opportunity these moments present. As an ancient parable teaches, rather than a taste of bitterness turning you sour, you smile knowing you've progressed one step further along the path of being all that you are.

* *Begin this practice by acknowledging that there is always a Power and Wisdom in your midst which is greater than your judgments about your personal failures. Centered in your heartspace, feel the loving embrace of this Transformative Presence throughout your being.*

* *Now inwardly open and ask this Presence moving through you to restore you to balance and sanity.*

* *Become aware of something you judge as a personal failure, past or present.*

* *Once you've identified it, what is the story you've created about it? What are the feelings you feel? Be honest.*

* *Turn the page now and recall a time you acted courageously. Feel that energy of courage in your body now from the top of your head to the soles of your feet.*

* *While remaining bonded to this energy of courage, move your attention to your heart. Centered there, choose to surrender your judgments and bitterness over this failure to the Greater Power and Wisdom within you. Feel the*

*Ed Conrad*

*release like a rushing wind sweeping through your soul.*

*Now inwardly ask this question: "What wisdom and inspiration may I gain from this past choice I have judged as a failure?" Stay with the question in your heart today and in the days to come. See what comes.*

# Sacred Geometry Meditation

*"Geometry existed before the creation."*

—Plato—

As a child you were exposed to either the wisdom or ills of previous generations. As an adult you may still feel tethered to the abrasive burn of certain childhood sounds, words, and events by a seemingly overpowering gravitational pull.

Or, you've been able to mentally and emotionally dissect your childhood, largely keeping only what inspired you to grow in love and wisdom. You discovered ways to be the spiritual architect of a new inner geometry and rebirth in spite of your childhood experiences.

Here's a subtle, but deeply effective tool for becoming more centered and less affected by the winds of emotional chaos. It assists in redesigning your inner geometry into a spectrum of consciousness which inspires and reveals new visions of possibility. Nothing in your inner life is set in stone.

* *Find a geometric design or symbol which speaks to your heart. There are so many wildly intricate and beautiful ones. One is the "sri yantra" geometric design which includes almost all shapes.*

* *Visually meditate at the very least for three minutes today on a geometric shape which appeals to you. Do your best to stay heart-centered while gazing at the symbol. Notice your inner experience which flows from this visual meditation. Repeat today as often as you like.*

PRACTICE #12

# Heartfulness

*"Love and compassion are necessities, not luxuries.*
*Without them, humanity cannot survive."*

—The Dalai Lama—

We are all flawed human beings. When you take the risk of letting others see your flaws and they accept you as you are, your shadow of self-judgment recedes. This simple act of heartfulness is seeing with the heart of compassion. The listener understands that the imperfections revealed by another are also within him.

> *On this day, take on this graceful heart of compassion and extend it to every-one you encounter. This selfless action is a balm for despair whether yours or someone else's. There is no greater cause. Give and it shall be given to you.*

PRACTICE #13

# Please Release Me

*"...before I can live with other folks I've got to live with myself."*

—Harper Lee, *To Kill a Mockingbird*—

Living out of integrity is a jarring speed bump many of us hit repeatedly. Stuck on this edge of existence, life feels unlived and unfulfilling.

❋ *Admit to the Divine Presence or a trusted person the ways you are living out of integrity, whether it is one isolated event, a longtime pattern of behavior, or both. Do this because you desire to be your true self. Freedom comes from not hanging on any longer to these patterns which do not serve you or anyone else.*

❋ *Your vulnerability and self-honesty must truly be from your heart. Nothing else has lasting effect. You do it for you.*

*Ed Conrad*

PRACTICE #14

# Down-To-Earth Wisdom

*"Under any circumstance, simply do your best, and you will avoid self-judgment, self-abuse and regret."*

—Don Miguel Ruiz, *The Four Agreements*—

American and other western cultures are obsessed with winning. So-called winners are adored and idolized. Fans are brokenhearted or deeply disappointed when their team is on "the wrong end of the score," or their idols fail to meet their high expectations.

These cultural obsessions with winning and subjective scales of success often come home to roost. You may be measuring yourself with these same scales.

Consider that your life is not a contest or competition. Ease up from the tendency to measure yourself as either a winner or loser.

Walk the middle path of the heart, which abandons the scales of judgment that certain cultures and philosophies tend to use to marginalize someone's value including your own.

* *Take to heart this down-to-earth wisdom which I learned early in life from my father who coached young people: "Play your best, look out for your teammates, and have fun." It applies to life wherever you are, whatever you're doing.*

* *Listen to the heart of the child that still beats within you and truly wants everyone to be loved and valued just as they are. May these four words stay with you like a mantra: play, best, teammates, fun.*

# Crossovers

*"Perhaps all the dragons in our lives are princesses who are only waiting to see us act, just once, with beauty and courage."*

—Rainer Maria Rilke, *Letters to a Young Poet*—

The art of living with heart is to feel fear but choose to not allow it to stop you from participating in the fullness of life.

As spiritual beings having a human experience, our calling is to crossover from fear to love, from fear to creative action, from fear to inner peace, from fear to appreciation, etc; and encourage and inspire our friends and loved ones to do the same.

The more crossovers you make, the more fear recedes into the backwaters of your life.

* *Take the time to become connected to your heartspace.*

* *Choose one of these crossovers to attend to today. The key is to acknowledge the fear or old story and keep going toward what it is that you truly want or need to express and experience.*

* *Apply this chosen crossover as often as possible today. Here's an example: In every situation today that you feel fear or hesitancy and the corresponding chatter from the voice inside your head, no matter what the voice or feeling of fear is communicating, take a step of action which would support what you want to create. While doing this, remain connected to your heartspace.*

* *Imagine this crossover as an opening you are moving through, not a solid barrier.*

PRACTICE #16

# Path of Non-Resistance

*"...you can use anything—everything—as a wake-up call; you can find a treasure trove of information about yourself and the world."*

—Elizabeth Lesser, *Broken Open: How Difficult Times Can Help Us Grow*—

The well-known spiritual teacher Krishnamurti was once asked, "What is the secret to your happiness?" He answered, "I don't mind what happens." Being in resistance to what takes place often prolongs pain, suffering, and confusion.

Chasing after the tail of why something happened or who's to blame or exacting justice always prolongs the hurt and keeps you stuck in painful loops of reactive nonsense. What matters is staying in contact with the feelings moving through you and being responsive to how to return to your center.

End your struggle against what happens. You will become increasingly alive rather than having your life energy siphoned away. It takes a great deal of energy every day to resist. You know this.

Let go of your end of the rope today. What does this mean? Rather than hiding, avoiding, or projecting onto others the turmoil within you, be present to what you are truly feeling by letting go of your resistance.

Begin establishing emotional literacy and intelligence in your life by becoming aware of what you are feeling.

* *Stay attuned with your heartspace throughout your day via heart-connected breathing.*

* *Notice when you are reacting to interactions and events of the day. Stay awake to what you are feeling in these moments rather than automatically letting your reactive, judgmental, fearful mind take over and keep you from being present to what you feel. Simply ask yourself, "What am I feeling?" Breathe and stay heart-connected and let the identity of your feeling come to you. Be present with it; not reacting from it.*

* *Resist not. This is the way of the heart.*

*Ed Conrad*

PRACTICE #17

# Empowering the Gold of Kindness and Generosity

*"In the end, maybe it's wiser to surrender before the miraculous scope of human generosity and to just keep saying thank you, forever and sincerely..."*

—Elizabeth Gilbert, *Eat, Pray, Love: One Woman's Search for Everything*—

Inherent in today's commitment is Mahatma Gandhi's insistence "to appeal to one's heart." Cease using the past as a reason to be unkind.

May today's practice inspire you to reimagine the whole of your life and get your aspirations and actions aligned with your most treasured personal and spiritual values.

* *Be still and center your attention in your heart and the rhythm of your breath.*

* *While in this rhythm, gently bring the golden rule into your awareness. "Do unto others, as you would have them do unto you." Repeat these words silently several times. Feel the power and compassion in these words.*

* *Completely drop your need to be right or superior or judgmental. Approach all beings and circumstances with equanimity and generosity.*

PRACTICE #18

# Create a New Story

*"...in Bilbo's heart: a glimpse of endless unmarked days without light or hope of bet-*
*terment...All these thoughts passed in a flash of a second. He trembled. And then*
*quite suddenly in another flash, as if lifted by a new strength and resolve, he leaped."*

—J.R.R. Tolkien, *The Hobbit*—

What have been the old disabling storylines of your life which you've been telling yourself for many years? They likely are an outgrowth of your emotional content and meaning-making of specific events and life choices which you believe have lead to specific predictable outcomes.

Here's an example: "Because of who I am and bad choices I've made, the ones I love inevitably leave me. I end up alone."

I share with you the following simple practice. It's not easy to do without getting stuck in persistent judgments. Go ahead anyway. It will help you reframe your stories and begin to experience the inspiring story of being you, the you your heart knows.

* *Write down an abridged version of the disabling storylines of your life.*

* *Close your eyes and let your breathing become full, effortless, and heart-centered. Keep your attention on your breath while placing one hand over your heart.*

* *Now, bring the whole of your life experience into your heartspace. Yes, all of it...Everything you have passed through from birth to this moment. It helps to have a simple object like a small ball represent your whole life. If you have one, caress it in both hands. If you don't have one, see it and hold it lovingly in your mind's eye.*

* *In this sacred, heart-centered consciousness, choose to lay to rest the dis-abling, shaming aspects of the old storylines. It's time. You're ready. Sit or move for several minutes if that feels right and acknowledge that within and around you is a power assisting you in this release.*

*Now, while in the awareness of the power of your heart and its electromagnetic field of energy, open to the realization that your life experience reveals your resilient spirit, your willing heart, your resolve that love would find you. Take this realization into your heartspace.*

*Resilience, willingness, resolve, love...these things you remember and hold in your heart in this moment. These are the themes of your new story beginning now.*

PRACTICE #19

# Be a Healing Presence

*"We are in each other's lives in order to help us see where we most need healing, and in order to help us heal."*

—Marianne Williamson, *Return to Love*—

Emotional and psychological wounds that recur can be tenacious especially the ones which first occurred before age four. They seem to pop up almost automatically under certain circumstances. They have no mercy and simply respond to stimuli which mimic the original wound. It feels at times like injustice. Something happens to you over which you seem to have no control.

An amplified deep resonance with your heartspace is a way to provide a soothing balm when these imprints become inflamed. Be a healing presence in your own life.

The following simple heart-centered meditation is an example:

* *Place both hands over your heart with the left hand on top of the right, thumbs touching.*

* *After a few moments of concentrated attention on your breath and heart-hand connection, say slowly this simple mantra: "Healing love come...come... come." Repeat this mantra several times in intervals of fifteen to twenty seconds. Spend at least three to four minutes in this resonance.*

*Ed Conrad*

# Turn Toward What You Deeply Love

*"Sometimes you hear a voice through the door calling you…*
*This turning toward what you deeply love saves you."*

—Jalaluddin Rumi—

What if you are truly living and creating a life you love? What if? Over the years, in a thousand ways, one piece at a time, your spiritual essence has revealed to you what the mosaic of your authentic life would look like.

It's never too late to turn toward what you deeply love. Settling for anything less only perpetuates a self-inflicted wound.

*Get a hold of this moment. Center your breathing in your heartspace and become still. Reconnect with your spiritual core, your heart-of-hearts.*

*In your inner awareness, imagine the door to your past is closing behind you. Give thanks that your past is complete. Acknowledge and feel this truth from the top of your head to the soles of your feet.*

*Turn your gaze in a new direction. In front of you is a new door. Feel the anticipation of something new coming to you. Open the door into your new life, into what you truly love, and who you truly are. Visualize closing this new door behind you.*

*Your new life is in front of you now. Ask your true spirit to fill you with love for your life. In this energy of love, see and feel yourself loving your life. What are you creating? What are you feeling? Spend 5-10 minutes in this sensory experience of being authentically you. Soak it in.*

# Calling Your Circle of Help

*"They say there is a place where dreams have all gone...It's miles through the night just over the dawn on the road that will take me home."*

—Mary Fahl—

Dreams remind you that you're not alone. It is as if you are in an overnight school of learning led by a guiding presence who is choreographing anecdotal tales with obvious and hidden messages. This presence assists you in finding your way through all things including your dark shadows.

This is one ongoing example of the many helpmates who hover within our subconscious awareness as well as nearby.

※ *Envision and feel your heart and mind energetically connecting in the center of your chest.*

※ *In this oneness of being, call all your personal and transcendent spiritual resources and helpmates together to assist and guide you through this day and the days to come.*

※ *This circle of help reminds you that wherever you are, you are not alone. Receive the strengthening energy of this truth into your whole being.*

# Pressing the Pause Button

*"For what it's worth: it's never too late or, in my case, too early to be whoever you want to be. There's no time limit, stop whenever you want. You can change or stay the same, there are no rules to this thing."*

—Eric Roth, *The Curious Case of Benjamin Button* Screenplay—

Your collective longing for time to stand still is expressed and experienced in so many powerful ways: paintings, photographs, songs, sculptures, architecture, deep silence, holding a gaze into another's eyes, inspired words, pure love.

You yearn to press the pause button. You want to feel being at the center of something beautiful and true and capture it in such a way that it would place an everlasting mark on your soul.

* *Don't let today pass by without pressing the pause button several times.*

* *Throughout your day, allow your eyes and your heart to fall upon something beautiful. Experience it as the spirit of eternal love joining alongside to inspire and gently remind you to appreciate being here.*

PRACTICE #23

# Circle of Outreach

*"I love you without knowing how, or when, or from where."*
—Pablo Neruda—

Connections are the juice of life. Appreciate when a friend turns their compass in your direction. Circles of love expand. Synchronicities occur. Stuck places loosen. The membrane that separates you from the world around you opens up more. The painful wounds of past transgressions are soothed.

When you extend love to a stranger or remembered friend, there is no end to the good which can fall into your lap.

> *Who could you turn your inner compass toward today? How about someone you don't know or someone you haven't reached out to in a long time? Place that call or send that message. Let your heart pour out to another. Let your circle of outreach grow.*

*Ed Conrad*

PRACTICE #24

# Become the Sky

*"You are the sky. Everything else – it's just the weather."*
—Pema Chödrön—

Today, may your spirit soar out and up with the eagle. It's necessary on occasion to forget where you are. Sometimes, you become too gravity prone.

* *Centered in your heartspace, take several slow, deep breaths. With each breath, gradually release all tension you may be holding in your shoulders and neck. Feel the release. Continue that release with each breath until your body feels fully relaxed.*

* *Sense the energy of expansion taking place as you shift your full attention to the energy field extending out from your heart. Stay attuned to this experience of you as heart energy. Your mind and nervous system are completely at ease.*

* *Now, depending on where you are, slowly stand up, if you can safely. Sitting is certainly fine, if you can't stand. Keep your attention on your experience of yourself as energy. If it's doable, raise your arms, and from your heart say a simple prayer to lift your spirit. Become the sky. You are the vibrant energy of vast space and the living expression of your prayer.*

* *After a few more moments, gradually let your arms come down and bring your hands together over your heart. Be fully present in the awareness that you are so much more than your physical body. You are the spirit of all life.*

# Flowing

*"May what I do flow from me like a river, no forcing and no holding back,*
*the way it is with children."*

—Rainer Maria Rilke—

Sometimes you cannot run or hide from the fact that you have too tight of a controlling grip on your life. You suffer the stressful effects.

You may tire a bit of hearing the four words "go with the flow." Yet, you must admit they contain a powerful truth. It is almost always harmful to habitually push back, resist, and consciously or unconsciously attempt to control everything which enters your sphere of life. You know this.

* *Let your mind and reactive brain dissolve into your heartspace. Become still and quiet.*

* *Imagine yourself being much more like a flowing stream. Hear the sounds of flowing water in your inner awareness. Like a fish in moving waters, feel the ease of movement of your breath and release of any resistance. Notice the changes. Sit quietly in this flow.*

* *Even though you may not know what lies ahead, you do what comes naturally for all streams; free of resistance, you flow over, around, and through what lies in front of you. Let go. Be effortless.*

* *Your heart, brain, and nervous system are now synchronized together as one coherent energy system. Pay close attention to the sensations and quality of awareness and ease. Return to this awareness throughout your day.*

PRACTICE #26

# Homage to the Bright Moons

*"Anyone can light a candle, but not the way that you do."*
—Jon Anderson—

Return to love. It is still there within you, even if you've exiled it to a hard-to-find place. To paraphrase a well-known teaching: It is better to express the love in your heart and risk loss than to close your heart and never open to love again.

* *Light a candle. Sit nearby. As your breathing slows and deepens, connect with your heart. Keep your focus on the light of the candle.*

* *Take time to pay homage to those who have been bright moons shining upon the waters of your life's journey. It could be the first 5-10 people who come into your awareness. While maintaining your visual focus on the light of the candle, connect with the spirit of each person and how they have touched your life. Let this time be a rich deepening of appreciation for all the ways you have experienced the shining light of wisdom and love in your life.*

* *Be still and know in your whole being that you are born to savor the fruits of the power of love. Feel the presence of love in your heart and allow it to expand throughout your body and beyond.*

* *When you feel ready, bring this ritual to a close. Love is with you always.*

# Awaken the Energetic Heart

*"If one advances confidently in the direction of his dreams, and endeavors to live the life which he has imagined, he...will pass an invisible boundary; and...live with the license of a higher order of beings."*

—Henry David Thoreau, *Walden*—

Scientific research confirms that the electromagnetic field of both the heart and brain are measurable. The electromagnetic energy of the heart extends at least five to eight feet beyond the physical body and, when measured, has been found to be one hundred to one thousand times stronger than the electromagnetic energy of the brain.

How do you tap the transformative benefits of this energy field? Learn how to experience yourself as energy. In western spiritual traditions, this would be called your spirit. In Hindu philosophy it's called prana. This dimension of being you, when activated, fine tunes your vibrational frequency. There are calming and transcendental effects and more.

* *First, close your eyes and center your attention and breath on the area in and around your physical heart.*

* *Once you feel relaxed, present, and heart-connected, which may take a minute or more, expand your awareness and imagine and feel your energetic heart as a powerful electrically and magnetically charged vibration encircling you.*

* *Silently repeat, "I am much more than my physical body. I am the vibration of heart energy. I am the spirit of life."*

* *Feel your whole body immersed in this presence and its subtle buzz and vibration. Charge yourself this way for at least 5-10 minutes.*

# Turn on Your Ahhhhh

*"Keep on walking. Keep on..."*
—J. D. Martin—

The word disaster literally means "from a star." Personal or collective disasters can either shut you down or pry you open into becoming a person who is inspired to breakthrough old fears. Yes, a disaster or crisis can wake you up from your apathy and powerlessness. You've likely already experienced this to some degree or another.

Rather than being apathetic and waiting for a sudden event to stir you to take hold of the mantle of your life, start today and commit to a steady non-violent path of persistent practice.

Here's an excellent example of turning up the wattage of light in your cells, which greatly helps to release the effects of stress and trauma in your body.

- *Sit quietly for several minutes breathing slowly in and out through your heart.*

- *Then after a full inhale, on the exhale chant out loud the sound "ahhhhh." Let the sound stretch out for at least 10-15 seconds. Do this repeatedly for each exhale for two minutes. Keep your mental attention on your heart. Ah is the sound of creating something from nothing.*

- *Now, make this shift. Each time you sound the "ah" on an exhale, feel a current of energy flow from your heart to the base of your spine connecting you with the earth which supports you. Then, with each inhale, feel the flow of energy from the base of your spine up to your heart, and with each exhale feel the energy flow from your heart back to the base of your spine and into the earth.*

- *Vibrating with this sound and feeling this flow, your body becomes a tuning fork. Tensions and anxieties will break apart. Stay with this for as long as you like.*

PRACTICE #29

# Shame-Free

*"The kingdom of God is within you."*

—Jesus of Nazareth—

Feelings of shame can become long-standing and self-destructive. No one benefits. Often the outcome of heart-powered practices and the like is to create an inner connection with your true spirit, your heart-of-hearts. In this inner temple of eternal truth, love is permanent and no shame exists.

* *Pause today. Feel and envision the energy of a warm radiating golden light between your navel and heart. Keep your full attention there. This light energy is your essence, pristine and shame-free. Let it expand and radiate throughout your whole being.*

* *See and feel the warmth of this golden light moving up through your heart and up to the spot between your eyes, sometimes called your third eye. Let this light radiate there. The frontal cortex of your brain is now activated and this golden light shines out to the world around you.*

* *Sit or stand in this shame-free state of radiating light for at least three minutes. Yes, the presence of divine light is shining within you and out into your world. Feel the electricity of your heart-brain connection enlightening you throughout your day.*

*Ed Conrad*

# Empower the Unknown

*"The moment one definitely commits oneself, then Providence moves too."*
—W. H. Murray—

Here's this year's special to-do list:

- *Move toward what you fear rather than away from it.*

- *Be less prone to accept someone else's version of truth.*

- *Challenge convention.*

- *Be energetically slippery, so fear can't easily hook you*

- *Inquire into mysteries, and let them flourish in you.*

- *Insist on answers being questioned.*

- *Open to undiscovered wisdom.*

- *Do not let this day go by without feeling profound appreciation for all you have discovered and passed through to be who you are now.*

- *Speak this question out loud with earnest: "What keeps any remaining walls of fear in me standing and what is required of me to take down these walls?" Sit quietly in heart-centered presence and hold this question in your awareness for several minutes. Make note of what comes to you.*

- *Ask your Higher Power to assist you in opening to receive the insight you need.*

PRACTICE #31

# I Am Love

*"All we are is a result of what we have loved."*
—Wayne Muller, *How Then Shall We Live?*—

When we are witness to selfless acts of loving kindness or heroic effort, we're likely moved to tears. These acts of the heart trigger a deeply felt remembrance of the bond of love we share, which is encoded in our sacred connection.

※ *Set aside time today to become still, and while centered in your heart, consciously attune to this presence of ageless truth calling you to remember that "Love is at the center of everything." Repeat this like a prayer.*

※ *Feel yourself opening to this Love which belongs to the universe and you.*

*Ed Conrad*

# Transforming a Wound

*"The deepest hunger in life is a secret that is revealed only when a person is willing to unlock a hidden part of the self."*

—Deepak Chopra, *The Book of Secrets:*
*Unlocking the Hidden Dimensions of Your Life—*

To counter the effects of a disturbing event, use the "Freeze-Frame" technique developed by Doc Childre and The HeartMath Institute. It is simple and effective. An example of this technique is farther down this page.

Afterward you'll likely feel calmer. You may receive confirmation of something you already know, or you may experience a complete shift in perspective, seeing the event in a more balanced way.

You may not have any control over the event, but you do have power over your perception of it and how you feel in your body.

By practicing this technique consistently, disturbing events that have taken you to your knees could steadily lose their power over you. May freedom find you.

* *Recall a recent event in your life which was disturbing or upsetting.*

* *Once you've recalled this event, shift out of your head and focus on the area around your heart. Keep your attention there for at least ten seconds. Breathe normally with a slow, steady rhythm.*

* *Next, recall a positive experience or feeling you have had in your life. Re-experience it now. Try not simply to visualize it, but feel it fully in your body.*

* *Once you truly feel connected in your body to this positive time or feeling, ask this question from your heart: "What can I do re: this recent disturbing situation to make it different?" or "What can I do to minimize the stress I feel?" Listen to the response of your heart.*

*Ed Conrad*

PRACTICE #33

# Cast Your Soul to the Sea

*"If the doors of perception were cleansed,*
*everything would appear...as it is—infinite."*
—William Blake—

Whether it is science, spirituality, religion, or personal exploration, all endeavors seeking to understand the larger truths of our existence are born out of an innate yearning to follow the arc of the Infinite and discover our true nature and source.

Each day is a platform for casting your nets of curiosity farther out and bringing the spirit of the Infinite into your lap. This is downright practical because it brings all manner of previously untouched wisdom into play. Your molecules can be rearranged, your hopes ignited, your visions inspired, your fears dissolved. It's as if heaven enters your days.

*In quiet reflection this day, hold firmly in your heart this vision expressed in words: "My True Source is Infinite and disguised as me. All fears are tiny drops in a vast sea of possibilities within me. I release all that I Am into this great expanse of Spirit and endless discovery from which my beautiful new story is born today." Repeat this vision several times throughout your day.*

*Acknowledge that day by day your heart, mind, and energy are becoming more and more coherent through the consistent repetition of these practices.*

# Integration

*"Return again, return again, return to the land of your soul.*
*Return to who you are, return to what you are, return*
*to where you are born and reborn again."*

—Rabbi David Zeller—

The inner landscape of being centered in the present moment welcomes change, cherishes the altogether new, and embraces visions of a future full of promise.

The effect of consistently creating coherence between the energetic fields of the heart and the brain keeps you more firmly grounded in the present moment. Scientific research confirms that this electromagnetism induces feelings of compassion, disarms the triggers for negative emotions, and gives rise to acceptance or appreciation for what has been, what is now, and hope for what is to come. The soul in you is coming to life.

* *While breathing slowly into your heart, feel your whole body firmly supported by Mother Earth underneath your feet. Stay consciously aware of this connection for several moments.*

* *Next, like the confluence of two rivers, see and sense flows of energy coming together in your heartspace from your left (what you have gained and learned from your past) and from your right (future possibilities). This confluence generates a power plant of love, healing, and creativity flowing from your heart-of-hearts out into your community.*

* *Smile and let it flow today*

PRACTICE #35

# The 100 Love List

*"I propose we fall in love several times a day for the rest of our lives."*
—Matthew Fox—

* *A transformational tool you can use to effectively dissolve your mind's fearful obsessions is to make a list of one hundred things you personally love. Number from one to a hundred on a sheet of paper. Then pause for a few moments and center and breathe into your heart. Write your list. It may take you 1-2 hours or more.*

* *The act of writing the list is a self-induced therapy session. Keep a copy of this in your wallet, purse, desk drawer, bedside table, or on your personal altar. Using both sides of a 5x8 sheet of journal paper works well. When folded once or twice, it fits easily into a purse or wallet.*

* *When the voice inside your head begins to over-dramatize or obsess on fear, pull out this list and read it even if you only read the first ten.*

* *Better yet, when you start to read the list, slow and deepen your breathing and shift your mental attention from your head to your heart. This practice is very effective in transforming the moment.*

# You Feel Powerless and Need Help

*"If we want greater clarity in our purpose or deeper and more meaningful spiritual lives, vulnerability is the path."*

—Brene Brown, *Daring Greatly*—

When you're feeling powerless, it is often difficult to ask for the love and support needed to help heal your pain. It may seem easier to trudge ahead without taking the courageous step to ask for help, love, or support. You know what I mean.

Your ego does not want to relinquish control. The emotional brain and psychological conditioning generate judgments and fears in response to feeling threatened or stressed. Face it. Your brain/mind is sorely inadequate when attempting to solely manage your emotional and psychological vulnerabilities.

Ease your pain and uncertainty and establish emotional balance.

* *Give yourself a break. Turn to the compassion of the heart in your community. Seek out a safe, judgment-free space. It could be a trusted person or professional or support group. Ask them to hear your fears and vulnerable feelings without judgment.*

* *Also, regularly turn to your heart when feelings of powerlessness come over you. Ask that the right and perfect help come to you now.*

PRACTICE #37

# Heart-Centered Listening

*"You know, I have come to think listening is love, that's what it really is."*
—Brenda Ueland—

Often, the kernel of what's stuck deep inside of us comes out to be heard because we are loosened by the presence of a sensitive and loving listener. This creates powerful healing possibilities for both the speaker and the listener. It is like being bathed in the healing love of the Great Mother of All. There is magic in it.

* *Throughout your day, give the jewel of judgment-free, heart-centered listening to those you are with.*

* *Turn off your cell phones. Be fully present with no distractions.*

* *Put in writing what you learn from being a sensitive and loving listener today and how you can apply this learning to your daily life.*

PRACTICE #38

# The Blessing Way

*"Be a lamp, or a lifeboat, or a ladder. Help someone's soul heal."*
—Jalaluddin Rumi—

❋ *Close your eyes for a few moments and breathe deeply into your heartspace. When you feel all systems slowing down into a more restful place, gently lift both your hands to shoulder height, keeping them open and relaxed with palms facing forward in a position of blessing. This mudra or hand gesture is an ancient Middle Eastern form of blessing and meditation.*

❋ *Hold this gesture for a minute or two. Keep your attention on breathing slowly and deeply into your heart. Notice what you sense and feel.*

❋ *Now direct your conscious attention toward someone in your life who is present with you or someone you imagine in your mind's eye. While directing loving and generous intent toward this person, continue to breathe fully with your hands still in the position of blessing.*

❋ *Stay with this for a minute or more. Then complete your blessing meditation by bringing your hands together in front of your heart. Hold this sacred prayerful gesture for several moments with your full attention on the coalescence of hands and heart. Many blessings be upon you and those you bless.*

# Venture Beyond Your Edges

*"I want to know if you will risk looking like a fool for love, for your dream, for the adventure of being alive."*

—Oriah Mountain Dreamer—

Venture out to the edges of where you have been and look beyond. Be an instrument of the Great Spirit today. Live beyond your old edges and walls.

Remember, there is and always shall be a sovereign presence and power within you and each and every being which is greater than any worldly fear.

*In your mind's eye, see yourself walking on a very straight and narrow path. Use all your focus to stay on that path. The path finally ends at an edge. Standing on this edge, you peer over. To your shock, it is a bottomless abyss. You recoil. For reasons you don't understand in the moment, you know you can't turn around and go back.*

*You stand perilously on the edge with a voice in you screaming loudly to back up and get away from the edge, fearing that you could fall to your death. Calmly, yet firmly, another voice in you says, "Go ahead." This inner conflict goes on for a bit.*

*Eventually, fear's illusions recede and a wave of calm comes over you. Before you have another moment to think about it, you boldly step forward over the edge. What appeared to be an abyss transforms into a welcoming landing spot just below you. With ease, you softly land on both feet. Looking around in all directions you realize you can choose from a number of paths. Life opens wide before you. You feel joy and thanksgiving.*

*Afterward, spend a bit of time looking within yourself and open to what each aspect of this inner experience means to you at this particular moment of your life. (one straight and narrow path, the end of the path is the edge of a cliff, the abyss, the fear of falling to your death, the voice within which says*

*"Go ahead," the wave of calm coming over you, the step over the edge, a safe landing spot, choice of many paths) What does all of this reveal to you? Make written notes.*

*Ed Conrad*

PRACTICE #40

# Heart Appeal

*"Your ears thirst for the sound of your heart's knowledge."*
—Kahlil Gibran—

When confronted with difficult people in difficult moments, I am reminded of Mahatma Gandhi's teaching of satyagraha which literally means "holding to the truth."

Here are Gandhi's words: "It is never the intention of the satyagrahi to embarrass the wrongdoer. The appeal is never to his fear; it is, it must be, always to his heart... He (the satyagrahi) acts naturally and from conviction...Satyagraha is gentle, it never wounds. It must not be the result of anger or malice. It is never fussy, never impatient, never vociferous."

The secret to all this is to stand in your strength and stay in your heart. Moving through life in this way establishes a steady inner fulcrum to help with staying balanced when all the world around you has gone mad.

> *Today, follow Gandhi's proven practice. Become a satyagrahi. That is, whoever comes your way, "Appeal to their hearts not their fears. Act from conviction without anger or malice." This requires that you be heart-connected and have the courage on occasion to open your heart and extend your heart energy to another.*

> *Appealing to someone's heart is appealing to their humanity, a humanity steeped in their sacred and valued place in our world no matter appearances.*

# From a Particle to a Wave

*"Resentment is like drinking poison and then hoping it will kill your enemies."*
—Nelson Mandela—

Resentment is a revealing word. It is an inner disturbance, which is repeatedly being "resent" from your past to the present moment via a thought, belief, feeling, or memory. It then becomes calcified in consciousness at the cellular level, resistant to change, and contributes to illness or injury.

It is the nature of living organisms to create waves of new life, new cells, new visions, new viewpoints.

Remember, the heart is the transmitter. When thoughts and feelings move through the heartspace, they become much more effective in calming your nervous system and generating a lasting, healing effect. This is truly one of the treasures of the heart.

    ❋  *Take a few moments to become centered and relaxed in your heartspace. Get into your heart-centered presence and out of the judgments of your mind.*

    ❋  *Set a clear intention to dissolve right now any resentments you still hold toward anyone including yourself.*

    ❋  *Bring into your awareness a specific resentment you still harbor against yourself or someone else. Stay aware of this resentment, keeping it in the background. Now, with loving conviction and heart-powered energy, prayerfully repeat the following phrase at least seven times: "from a particle to a wave." This energizes a wave-like transmission that dissolves the remnants of resentment in the consciousness within your cells. Follow this phrase with "Resentment is dissolving now. Thank you." Repeat these powerful phrases over and over and over for several minutes or longer. Let your intuition guide you.*

PRACTICE #42

# Be a Potter

*"Mold me and make me after thy will, while I am waiting, yielded, and still."*
—Traditional Hymn—

Notice how potters "throw" pots on a potter's wheel. Once clay is centered on the wheel, it's still a lump of clay waiting for what's next. The potter's hands then act on the clay, pressing it down, digging into the heart of the clay and opening a well. The clay is then stretched out, making room for growth.

Like a potter, you need to have a nose for the center. There is a center to your life. To develop a nose for it, you may need to sit at your wheel for a bit.

* *That is, while you sit and notice the turnings of your mind, place your full attention on your heart. There, amid all these turnings, is your center. From your center, you're much more likely to discover what all potters and lovers know—the sacred art of opening.*

* *From this heart-centered state of consciousness, ask your Higher Power to open you like wet and stretchable clay in the hands of a master potter.*

* *Center, ask, open, and be shaped into something new.*

* *Then, it is as if an unseen presence begins to take what you see, what you think, how you feel, and who you are, and shape you into a new vessel.*

PRACTICE #43

# Healing Love

*"A thousand deaths my heart has died, and*
*thanks be to love, it lives yet."*

—Hazrat Inayat Khan, *The Dance of the Soul*—

The human experience at times feels fragile. I have looked into the eyes of parents who have lost children prematurely. No matter the cause, there is a depth of emptiness within them, which is unlike anything else. It is up to the community around them to be responsive and provide love and support in whatever ways are needed.

Take this to heart today: in truth, real love never dies.

* *Wherever you are right now, give a moment of heartfelt attention to those in your life who have lost a loved one whatever the reason. This could be you.*

* *Silently pour your heartfelt love into the Great Spirit which connects us and stirs us to love one another. Waste no time. Do this now.*

* *Make note in writing of the thoughts and feelings that come up when sending out healing love.*

# Power-Generator

*"You gain strength, courage, and confidence by every experience in which you really stop to look fear in the face."*

—Eleanor Roosevelt—

The inner crossroad of courage and fear is likely the busiest, most consequential intersection in your life. This clash is especially juicy when you need to rise up and put your life back together again after a personal downfall or broken relationship.

❋ *In this moment, establish a steady breathing rhythm slow and deep. Shift your focus to your heart.*

❋ *Make the inner journey to your favorite power-generator on the planet. It is a place, relationship, or activity which generates feelings of safety, courage, peace, inspiration, as if an Infinite Presence is close at hand. It could be a place in nature or in your home, or a significant relationship, or a form of self-expression which ignites self-confidence.*

❋ *Spend 3-4 minutes feeling and visioning your empowering connection with your power-generator.*

❋ *When fear arises today or anytime, shift your focus to your heart-center and re-establish your connection with your power-generator. Don't be shy or hesitant. Feel the surge of courage and energy in your whole being.*

❋ *Courage or fear...Which do you choose?*

PRACTICE #45

# Simple Presence

*"To attain knowledge, add things every day.*
*To attain wisdom, remove things every day."*

—*Tao Te Ching*, verse 48—

Ask yourself, "What needs to be removed?" Here's one possibility: Remove your mind's need to weave problematic mental and judgmental webs which block access to your deeper wisdom. The antidote to this persistent troublemaking habit of the voice inside your head is the practice of simple presence.

* *Simple presence is initiated by the practice of conscious connected breathing in which you place your attention on each inhale and exhale as they flow one into the other, continuing on through each and every breath.*

* *When your connected breathing is heart-centered, this practice is even more effective at removing the distraction of the voice inside your head.*

* *Today, each time the voice inside your head starts up, choose to gently shift to your simple presence practice.*

# Gathering Your Soul Family

*"To all my friends in far-flung places...when again I'll see your faces, no one knows, no one can say, and none can name that happy day."*

—Chuck Pyle—

* *Take time to be still while breathing slowly and effortlessly into your heart. Maintain your heart-centered breathing. One by one, bring into your mind's eye those loved ones past and present with whom you have had a valued connection.*

* *Make a list if you choose. Imagine all of them joining together in a sacred circle with you in the center.*

* *Once this circle of souls is complete, in your inner awareness, pour out your love and appreciation to each of them and speak their name. This is your soul family.*

* *Now, continue to see yourself in the center. Open to feel and receive from them their love for you. Cherish the love and connection binding you together always.*

PRACTICE #47

# See With the Heart

*"The secret is 'it is only with the heart that one can see rightly;*
*what is essential is invisible to the eye.'"*

—Antoine de Saint Exupéry, *The Little Prince*—

In the deepest understanding of your heart, you are seeking to experience life in its unified state. This is what we call love.

This inner realm of oneness is mostly hidden from you. So you seek it elsewhere in the world around you. As a result, at best, you get a ripple effect, the virtual reality of it, rather than the direct experience.

*See everything with the eyes of your heart today. Begin with the baseline understanding that everyone and everything you see are connected energetically and arise from one "unified field." You may choose to call it Spirit or God.*

*Centered in your heart/mind coherent connection, set your felt intention to have a direct experience of the invisible truth of life. Ask that all your senses be fine-tuned by the energy of your heartspace.*

*Keep the results of your experience close to your heart and let it feed your choices, prayers, and meditations. Make written note of what you "see" today.*

# Belonging

*"(It's a) real humdinger...that all organisms have descended...*
*from a single ancestral cell."*

—Franklin Harold, *The Way of the Cell*—

Because you have been born on this earth, you belong. You are hardwired for belonging.

The following daily practice of consciously connecting with feelings of belonging and acceptance strengthens what you are already hardwired to be. In the grand scheme of this endless universe, wherever you go, wherever you are, you are right where you belong. Welcome...

   ❋   *Today, identify a time and place and the people present in which you truly felt you belonged. You were welcomed into their lives with a genuine spirit of love and acceptance. This time and place could be occurring now. Visualize this now in your inner awareness.*

   ❋   *Centered in your heart, take time to recall and allow these feelings of belonging to come to you. Do this practice for at least 3-5 minutes today while standing. By standing and sensing your feet firmly supporting your whole self, you embody the spirit and energy of belonging. There is a place for you here.*

   ❋   *Make note in writing of your insights about your sense of belonging as you experience it in your life today.*

# Quantum Expansion

*"Listen to your life. See it for the fathomless mystery that it is."*
—Frederick Buechner—

Looking at points of distant light in the night sky registers a familiarity as if gazing into the eyes of a loved one. The infinite becomes intimate. You could say it is as if we are peering into ourselves and somehow remembering that light is our true nature and source.

* *Pause tonight and become centered in your heart. Imagine it as a powerful generator of light. While sitting or standing, with eyes closed, imagine beaming your heartlight across a room. Now extend that beam of light across town to someone you care about. Then expand even more, and extend your light across the country to someone you know and love.*

* *Finally, whether day or night, send your light and energy way out into space. See and feel the expansion of your whole being reaching to the moon, sun, or beyond. Stay with this for several minutes.*

* *Then shift and imagine and feel the light from deep space and your loved ones now shining upon you. You are in shining oneness with it all. Take it in.*

PRACTICE #50

# Spirit-Breath

*"For breath is life, and if you breathe well you will live long on earth."*
—Sanskrit Proverb—

The following conscious breathing practice transforms your breathing patterns into a powerful movement of Spirit-Breath. To the Christian mystic, this has been called the Holy Breath or the more familiar Holy Spirit. You are able to think more clearly, access your intuition more easily, stabilize your emotional states, help your body heal, and have more frequent flashes of inspiration.

* *Become aware of your breathing patterns. On the inhale, focus your attention on your navel. Then follow the expansive movement of your breath upward from your navel to your heart. On the exhale and release, follow the flow of your breath back toward your navel. The inhale flows like an uplifting wind and the exhale leaves you opened and relaxed.*

* *Do this breathing practice today for at least three one-minute periods. In these conscious, mini-breath sessions, make sure there is a full, soft, and deep flow. As mentioned before, breathe into the space between your navel and heart. Expand, then let go.*

PRACTICE #51

# What Flaws Reveal

*"I am not washed and beautiful, in control of a shining world*
*in which everything fits."*

—Annie Dillard—

You have flaws which are etched into your daily life. However, it is often the case that these flaws turn into revelations of wisdom and energy to shape your life in surprising ways. Rather than being your nemesis, your imperfections can be a catalyst to open you to surprises which lay underneath.

This twist in perception provides a clarifying lens through which hidden strengths come to light. May you discover the whole truth of who you are.

*Close your eyes and feel and breathe your way into your heartspace. Take a minute or two. Bring to your awareness a positive emotion such as appreciation and associate it with a relationship or experience you appreciate in your life right now. Let the energy of your heart and mind come into coherence. The rhythm of your heartbeat and the neurons firing in your brain are in sync.*

*Now, while remaining consciously connected to feelings of appreciation, bring into your awareness what you judge as one of your flaws. Stay with heart-connected breathing. Gradually notice how you see this flaw while in this state of heart/mind coherence. You may notice that it's like standing back from this flaw as if you're viewing an intricate work of art which has a flaw. You look closely with a discerning, compassionate heart.*

*When considering your flaw, how do you assess it? What do you feel about it? What are you discovering about yourself which this flaw reveals? Make note of what comes to you.*

*When seen with a heart of discernment and understanding, your flaws or shadows may reveal something quite surprising about yourself.*

*Ed Conrad*

# Your Heart of Power

*"Our deepest fear is not that we are inadequate. Our deepest fear is that we are powerful beyond measure...Your playing small does not serve the world."*

—Marianne Williamson—

When passing through the experience of brokenness, it is likely going to be fertile, raw, scary, and messy. These are the conditions for entry into a new dimension of life. You are like clay again with some old shards mixed in.

The Great Spirit has you given the hands and the heart to shape what remains. There is more to you than you can imagine.

> *Today, with your inner vision, see and imagine your heartspace extending several feet beyond your physical body in a full circle around you. Carry yourself through the day in this large way.*

> *Remember, the Spirit of the Divine Presence in you is powerful beyond measure! Use this power for a greater good today. Feel the grandness of being connected to your heart and the hearts of others.*

PRACTICE #53

# Deep Peace

*"Waiting to grasp the ungraspable, you exhaust yourself in vain. As soon as you relax this grasping, space is there...All is yours already."*

—Venerable Lama Gendun Rinpoche—

Yield to the flow of life. Insist on being the peace surpassing all understanding…just for today.

Imagine this peace leveling all ripples of disturbance. From this inner positioning flows creative action free of constraint. When you connect with this presence in you, you are living from the marrow of your life, from the seat of your soul.

* *Even amid the busyness of your day, at least twice take time and space to breathe deeply into your heart and stay centered there.*

* *Record the following simple guided meditation in your own voice and then play it back:*

  *Imagine floating upon a depth of calm waters. Let go and allow this buoyancy to gently support you. Feel completely relaxed from the top of your head to the soles of your feet. Within and all around is an undisturbed presence of effort-lessness. The gravity of life is dispersed. You are undisturbed presence. You are peace. Take this to heart.*

* *Sit in this depth of quiet and peace for as long as you choose.*

PRACTICE #54

# What You Value

*"Service is the rent each of us pays for living—the very purpose of life."*
—Marian Wright Edelman—

As a child and young man, I paid close attention to my grandfather. He was a practicing chiropractor for 64 years. His mission was to relieve the suffering of others. I often noticed he was very willing to say "yes" when someone was hurting and needing help. This value became my own.

Let what you truly value pull you forward into the rest of your life.

- *Write down three to five of your core values. An example is what I mentioned above: "To help relieve the suffering of others."*

- *Then, answer the question, "Aside from the possessions of my life, what is of greatest value to me now?" Make note of at least three to five aspects of your life which are of greatest value. An example might be, "Deep, loving connection with others."*

- *Compare these two lists. Notice that there may be some differences or similarities. Combine the two lists into one. Post this values list in your car and in a conspicuous place where you live. Let them be your ever-present inspiration for being you.*

# Practice #55
# Let a River Run Through

*"If we have no peace, it is because we have forgotten that we belong to each other."*
—Mother Teresa—

Life is an endless river with a strong current. As beings who live together in this current, we may fight against it and feel we need to fight against each other for our place.

Or, we learn to trust our symbiotic relationship with each other and the current that is our life support. We let go and open to its powerful energy supplying all that we could ever want or need. We remember that it is our nature to reach out and love and support one another. This is what we are here for.

We are the hearts. We are the hands. We are in this great river of life together as it carries us onward. This is what is true.

> *Come to an agreement with yourself today. Be your own heart monitor, a bold activist for your true voice. Listen from your heart. Speak from your heart. Don't let fear stop you. Be helpful to others and ask for help as well. That's it. Try it on.*

# Measure of Good

*"There, but for the grace of God, go I."*

—Unknown—

Turn your awareness toward those standing on local street corners or in food lines who are experiencing the powerlessness of isolation, injustice, or homelessness. Almost all of us connect with these shared human experiences at some level. Today, without pride or resentment, whatever your personal circumstances may be, acknowledge the measure of good which has come to you.

❋ *Without judgment or evaluation of how little or how much you have, open your heart in humble appreciation for the basics you receive: warmth, food, companionship, health of mind and body, clothing, love, freedom of movement, income, etc.*

❋ *In the midst of your feelings of appreciation, let your attention turn to someone you know who is struggling to have their basic needs met. Give them some room in your heart today as well. We are in this together. Better yet, take sincere action today to help someone in need.*

# Passion

*"I awake inside myself. It's like a flame forever burning or a diamond in a mirror turning or a cathedral when there's no one there."*

—Steven Walters—

There is a profound spiritual dimension to passion whether it is the yearning for sexual union with a loved one, the spirited enthusiasm to complete your life's work, the joy of doing what you love, or the mystical calling to join with the Infinite. All of us naturally desire to experience the blessings of passions fulfilled and end the pains of being disconnected and alone.

* *Find a window of time and space to sit quietly. Close your eyes and establish a rhythm of slow, deep breaths.*

* *Shift your attention to your sexual organs. Open to and feel any sexual stirrings. After several more deep breaths, gradually raise these sexual stirrings up into your heartspace. Feel this energetic connection between your heart, body, and sexuality.*

* *Humbly set the clear prayerful intention that all the passions of your heart, soul, mind, and body serve to strengthen the bonds of love and heal the pains of separation in every aspect of your life. Feel this prayer from the top of your head to the soles of your feet. Remember, have your prayerful intention be the embodied awareness of the deepening and expansion of you as energy.*

PRACTICE #58

# Tonglen

*"Imagine a Divine conversation in which you are asked
to help in some great endeavor."*

—Lance Secretan—

The following is one version of the ancient meditation practice of "tonglen." Be clear that you are participating in this sacred practice to be an instrument of healing the individual and collective suffering in our world. It begins with you and me and each and every single one of us. This is much needed. Doing this practice in groups can be especially potent. Thank you for participating.

　❋　*Begin by slowing your rate of breathing. Take full, long, deep breaths, inhaling and exhaling through your heart. Feel an inner calm and peace. Your heart and mind are now in coherence.*

　❋　*You are going to participate in a courageous act of compassion. While remaining centered in your heart, begin by acknowledging and attuning to human suffering. It helps to be specific. For example, turn your attention to the world's refugee crisis or something closer to home which reflects the profound pain of human suffering.*

　❋　*As you slowly inhale, take this suffering into your heart, only for the 5-7 seconds of each inhale.*

　❋　*Then, when slowly exhaling, breathe out healing love and compassion for our brothers and sisters and all living things wherever they may be.*

　❋　*Breathe in the suffering. Breathe out the feeling of healing love and compassion. Do this powerful practice for 3-5 minutes or longer if you choose. This can also be medicine for your own personal suffering.*

*Ed Conrad*

# Breathe Deeply and Fluidly

*"Feelings come and go like clouds in a windy sky.
Conscious breathing is my anchor."*

—Thich Nhat Hanh, *Stepping into Freedom:
Rules of Monastic Practice for Novices*—

Wind, air, and breath insure that all life is sustained. Breath is more than life sustaining. It can be a portal to Spirit, your source of inspiration and infinite possibility.

When you breathe deeply and fluidly, you are much more likely to live deeply and fluidly. Your spirit is awakened. It is like a cleansing wind blowing through a smog-filled valley. You move through life with greater ease and wisdom and become more akin to a dolphin than a mule-like beast of burden.

You are the fruits of the ways you breathe.

*Give consistent attention this day to your breathing patterns. Notice when you're holding your breath or breathing shallow or losing your breath.*

*Each time you notice one of these breathing aberrations, return to breathing more slowly and deeply through your nose while remaining consciously heart-connected.*

*Apply this especially when you sense stress or anxiety.*

# The Golden Cord of Forgiveness

*"Life is an adventure in forgiveness."*

—Norman Cousins—

Forgiveness is transformative medicine for what ails and paralyzes us. It provides a handle for us to firmly grasp the golden cord of life which is always interwoven with the love in our midst. This divine quality of love frees us from past impressions, heartbeat by heartbeat, breath by breath.

* *Throughout your day, as if he is speaking directly to you, hear these healing words which are reported to have been spoken by Jesus of Nazareth to a man who had been paralyzed and unable to walk for decades. "You are forgiven. Arise, take up the bed you've been lying on and go home." Upon hearing these words, the man stood up and walked home.*

* *Attune to what these words convey. Whatever you have been lying in which is paralyzing your true spirit and closing your heart, arise, and firmly take hold of the golden cord of forgiveness. Go where it is leading. There is nothing you have ever done which leaves you outside the presence of unconditional love. Nothing. Forgiveness is love in action.*

* *Take to heart the following declaration:"I arise and turn my full attention toward the vast irresistible expanse of awe-inspiring love and possibility I see and feel within me. Centered in my heart, I decisively cross over my threshold of fear and hesitation. With every movement and choice I make, the coherent energy of my heart, mind, and body is disconnecting me from every harmful emotional impression from the past. My old inner structure of survival, emotional paralysis, judgment, and fear is collapsing because the empowering luminous energy of love is being fully restored in me. The spirit and truth of me is clearer with every beat of my heart and every breath I breathe. I am now firmly on my heart-powered path."*

PRACTICE #61

# Express Your Love

*"Thank you for the true love you brought to me when it was time at last for words to come out of silence and take me by surprise."*

—W. S. Merwin, *Variations on a Theme*—

Too much of the time we keep our heartfelt feelings to ourselves. We don't express to those we truly love and appreciate that we love and care for them. Holding back serves no one.

❋ *Today, don't withhold what you feel. Express to someone close to you that you love them. Allow them to experience the power of what's in your heart. Be a catalyst for creating a more love-inspired world.*

*Ed Conrad*

PRACTICE #62

# Power Pose

*"What lies behind you and what lies in front of you,
pales in comparison to what lies inside of you."*

—Ralph Waldo Emerson—

There is a frequency, a way of moving through each day, that is your ground of being. You are open, emotionally balanced, energized, and courageous. You are immersed in being authentically you. Connect to this power.

- *Breathe into your heartspace and create a body pose which expresses who you have come here to be. Let it flow out of you. Hold this pose for a few moments. Feel it. Sound it out.*

- *Repeat this exercise. Take this energetic awareness with you today.*

- *Describe your authentic self in writing in as much detail as possible. What would you be doing which would leave you feeling open, emotionally balanced, energized, highly creative, and bold? What are the most valuable practices which would help you sustain your authentic life?*

PRACTICE #63

# Off the Hook

*(Sabbath is) "the presence of something that arises when we consecrate a period
of time to listen to what is most deeply beautiful, nourishing, or true."*

—Wayne Muller, *Sabbath*—

This is not a day or time of doing for doing's sake. Put to bed that compulsive presence which insists on getting things done. It's obsessed and exhausted and so are you.

I offer you this option today. This is traditionally saved for the weekly sabbath day. Any day or timeframe will do.

&ast; *Take a sabbath. What I mean is, take yourself off the hook. Consecrate a period of time to cease and desist from all practices that support the need to change something about yourself, make your mark on the world, and/ or accomplish some task. Turn your cell phone off and set aside any other devices which distract you from being present with yourself and others.*

&ast; *I am suggesting a day-long sabbath. If you insist this is too long, then do an eight hour sabbath.*

&ast; *Abide in your heart. Feel your light. Simply be and what you truly need will come to you like a bee to nectar.*

PRACTICE #64

# A Grateful Heart

*"This is life in all its glory, swirling and unfolding around us,
disguised as pedantic, pedestrian non-events."*

—Shauna Niequist, *Cold Tangerines:
Celebrating the Extraordinary Nature of Everyday Life*—

Gratitude truly is a causative energy and source of vitality which ignites greater creativity and energy.

If your grateful heart keeps on giving thanks, not out of obligation, but simply out of the recognition that every day is a gift, you are certain to experience even more to be grateful for. You have a decided choice how to color your life. Tap this resource today.

- *Refine your visual, mental, and emotional focus, so that you are experiencing your life today through the lens of being grateful. Tapping the energy of the heart through consistent attention on heart-centered breathing will assist in actually seeing with a grateful heart.*

- *Keep a running list. You are putting together a one-day gratitude journal.*

# Opening

*"The most beautiful people we have known are those who have known defeat, known suffering, known struggle, known loss, and have found their way out of the depths."*

—Elisabeth Kubler-Ross—

You have withstood life's tests but not without scars and thundering movements of grief. Through these woundings and releases, you have crossed a wasteland inside. Your heart touches the bitterness of loss and the bare powerless reality of staring into the unfamiliar.

These crossings are where the greatest challenges lie. Your choice is to close and contract into the fear and pain of loss, or, even with the wound and suffering, to remain open.

⁕ *One of the classic nervous system responses to fear is to freeze. Notice today where you may be contracted, afraid, or frozen. Bring that feeling into your heartspace. Breathe into this moment with the intent to open.*

⁕ *Then declare firmly out loud, "Photons of light within every cell of my body are now turned on and beaming into every scared and closed place of my being, opening me to receive and feel the healing presence and frequency of love." Repeat while staying in your heartspace.*

⁕ *Relax, breathe slowly and deeply, and give thanks for the energy and frequency of light which is everywhere present within and around you. You are a manifestation of the light of the stars.*

PRACTICE #66

# Active Heart-Centered Reflection

*"I make the effort to see the Beloved in everyone
and to serve the Beloved through everyone."*

—Ram Dass—

Periodically words are needed less and quiet reflection is needed more, especially in these times of reactive emotional and collective intensity.

Heart-centered connection and reflection helps to declutter and calm the mind. Mind-centered reflection often does not.

Through heart-centeredness, everyday life becomes more like an active empowering meditation and less like an ego-driven, anxiety-creating performance.

* *In your interactions today, allow more moments of heart-centered reflection and connection. As quoted in a previous practice, "appeal to people's hearts."*

* *Let this ride throughout your day. Trust it. Your focus shifts from disconnected, auto-pilot, rote responses to simple attention on authentic, present-moment, heart-connected spontaneity.*

PRACTICE #67

# The Mind in the Heart

*"To begin to draw the juice from the new fruits that are ready to ripen in your life, visualize and feel the heart and mind becoming one."*

—Ed Conrad, *Heart Power*—

Simple mind-in-the-heart meditations open an inner gate to transformational possibilities. These tools are designed for the mind and heart to coherently join with one intention, rather than operating in a state of separation.

The script of your new heart/mind coherence can be written and put into action. It replaces the old pattern of either your mind acting alone and endlessly obsessing on old fears and judgments or your heart acting alone and desperately seeking to find fulfillment and love.

* *Visualize and feel your mind dropping and merging with your heart. Breathe slowly and deeply with your awareness centered in this union of heart and mind.*

* *From this union of heart and mind, ask the question, "Who would I be if I chose to consciously and consistently create a coherent partnership of heart and mind?" List at least three possibilities which would result. See and feel new beginnings knocking at your door.*

84 *Ed Conrad*

PRACTICE #68

# Intervals of Silence

*"You can talk with someone for years, everyday, and still, it won't mean as much as what you can have when you sit in front of someone, not saying a word, yet you feel that person with your heart..."*

—C. JoyBell C.—

There is an urgency drawing many of us toward silence. Like listening to beautiful poetry which flows with a rhythm of words and silence, we are urged to listen with our hearts. There we hear refrains of wisdom and peace echoing from a deeper awareness which could be summarized with these words: "Stop the endless noise. Receive the power of silence."

The following practice is designed to nurture your connection to the still small voice centered within your heart.

*I invite you to use this day as a testing ground for keeping your inward attention on your breath and heartspace. Maintain this focus even when you are hearing with your ears what others are saying to you.*

*Keep your vocal expressions to a minimum. Feel the gift of silence and stillness flow around and through you.*

PRACTICE #69

# Arms of Love

*"I will soothe you and heal you. I will bring you roses.*
*I too have been covered with thorns."*

—Jallaludin Rumi—

Kindness and mercy toward ourselves are often missing. Yet, if the chance presented itself, you'd run as fast as possible and throw yourself into the arms of Amma, the hugging saint, or Mother Theresa, or Jesus, or Kwan Yin, the Buddhist goddess of compassion, crying out to have all your dark and unhealed places taken from you. You long to feel this divine healing embrace of unconditional love and mercy.

❋ *Who would you want to hold you in this way? Choose who it would be.*

❋ *Whoever it is, real or imagined, go ahead and satisfy your inner longing. See yourself standing in front of this being of love and compassion.*

❋ *Feel your heart opening and your walls coming down. Let go of all resistance. Fall into their arms. Open your whole self to receive their full embrace. Feel their arms holding you and their wholehearted love flowing through you...a love that heals, a love that sets you free...only love.*

❋ *Whatever wants to come out of you, let it come. Only love is with you now.*

*Ed Conrad*

PRACTICE #70

# Spiral of Creative Energy

*"I live to feel this lightning in the perfect storm where earth and heaven meet."*
—David Wilcox—

True inspiration is about feeling your connectedness to the Great Spirit of the universe and its infinite, immeasurable, dazzling qualities. This Great Spirit is not something you control. You draw from it in order to celebrate being human. An inspired human who truly lives to serve the greater good in this world is as divine as unconditional love.

* *Become still and quiet. Bring simple attention to your breath. For a few moments, breathe slowly into that spot about two fingers below your navel. This helps you feel grounded and solid.*

* *Now bring to your awareness an issue needing to be resolved or a choice needing to be made.*

* *With your attention centered in your heart and eyes closed, sense and feel that all your inner and outer resources are joining together to inspire you— one spiral of illuminating, creative energy. As you move through what lies in front of you, this kinetic dynamo is surrounding and infusing you with inspiration and courageous resolve.*

* *Feel your resolve and strength. Give thanks.*

* *Put in writing the guidance you are receiving. Stay in your heart.*

# A Great Reservoir

*"Without a generous heart there can be no true spiritual life."*
—Buddha—

Like a well-known parable teaches, become more like a great reservoir than a glass of water. Put a teaspoon of salt in a glass of water, and the water tastes bitter. Put that same amount of salt in a great reservoir, and the water still tastes sweet.

* *Bring your attention to the left center of your chest. Become heart-connected.*

* *Take precious time today to breathe into and feel the expansive electromagnetic field stretching out from your physical heart like the swell of a tidal surge. Attune to the power of this energy all around you. It is your reservoir of generosity and sweet possibility in which bitterness is dissolved.*

* *Be the reservoir not the glass. How would this metaphor manifest in your life?*

* *Put your thoughts in writing.*

# Overriding the Brain

*"Follow your heart and make it your decision."*

—Mia Hamm—

If your brain/mind largely dominates your day-to-day choices, when difficult emotions arise, you can often get caught in the web of the brain's fearful responses and overreactions. You likely tend to withdraw, freeze, or react.

Remember, there is a mind in your heart. You can choose to use this inner resource and "heartfully" respond to life's circumstances. This approach moderates the brain's impulse to fight, avoid, harshly judge, or freeze.

Rather than being controlled by the automatic fearful responses of your emotional or reptilian brain, your heart sends a message to those parts of your brain to calm down. You are safe and ok.

From this simple heart-directed shift, a very different set of possibilities becomes available to you.

*When your brain triggers a fearful or anxious response in your nervous system, stop and redirect your attention and make a conscious connection with your heart. Breathe into your heart more slowly and deeply with each breath. Choose to let the power of your heart lead.*

*Use this simple shift of attention today each time you are aware that your brain and nervous system are triggered.*

*What do you notice when you use this simple shift of attention? Put it in writing.*

PRACTICE #73

# Overturning Judgment

*"You yourself, as much as anybody in the entire universe,*
*deserve your love and affection."*

—Sharon Salzberg—

Science and ageless wisdom teachings confirm that holding feelings and thoughts of critical judgment about yourself or another create not only harmful biochemical and neurological effects in your body, they also disturb your spiritual core.

I leave it to the deep wisdom abiding in you to end your habits of harsh judgment. The secret is staying heart-connected. There the truth is known and felt and will lead you into right action where love, partnership, bold action, and healing take place. Your life is becoming a daily experience of making consistent shifts from reactive nervous system responses to heart/brain coherence.

* *Set your heart on being free this day of the corrosive pattern of judging others and yourself.*

* *If judgment or irritability begins to arise, shift your conscious attention to heart-centered breathing. Notice what takes place in your body.*

PRACTICE #74

# Turn on the Light

*"Is it true that our destiny is to turn into light itself?"*

—Hafiz—

Many are magnetically drawn to holding a newborn very close. It feels like basking in the sun. You perceive a radiance, a halo effect which is irresistible.

For those few moments you believe an angel of light has been sent to soften what has become hardened inside you. While still holding the child, someone says to you, "you look different."

* *If you have a picture of you as a baby or very young child, connect with it today. If you don't have a picture, remember a time and place in your inner awareness when you were age six or younger. Recall what you can about you as this child.*

* *Settle into your heart for a moment and breathe deeply. Hold vigil for this child in you. Carry this image of you as a small child in your heart and mind today. See your face. Feel your light and warmth and the spirit and wonder moving through you.*

* *Prayerfully centered in your heart, ask to be opened and guided in ways that turn on the light you were born to be.*

* *Put in writing what would turn on your light more consistently each day. Remember, you can actually activate the light at the quantum level of being.*

PRACTICE #75

# Everyday Sabbath

*"Your sacred space is where you can find yourself over and over again."*
—Joseph Campbell—

Life is so often about balance and taking complete care of your soul and body. Settling all the way into a restful, uninterrupted state of consciousness soothes the soul, restores the nervous system, and calms the inner chatter. The following is a ritual of keeping the Sabbath every day and literally being an instrument of peace.

* *As always, become still and breathe into your heartspace and give the chatter inside your head a rest. You are benefitting from heart/mind coherence.*

* *Settle all the way into deep restoration today for a brief block of time, 2-3 minutes minimum. Let go all the way. Sense and feel the vibration of being you free of distraction. If reasonable this day, do this restoration practice several times.*

*Ed Conrad*

PRACTICE #76

# Heart-Generated Energy

*"HeartMath research confirms our intuitive understanding of the heart with solid science and explains how the electromagnetic field radiating from the heart can affect those around us."*

—Doc Childre, *The HeartMath Solution*—

Attune to your heart-generated energy system. Your physical heart beats on average about 90,000 times every 24 hours supplying life blood to your body. It's an astonishing, entirely unconscious activity.

⁜ *Several times today spend at least one minute with your full attention feeling your pulse. Become conscious of the beating of your heart.*

⁜ *Secondly, focus your conscious attention and breath on your heartspace. Like a light extending its rays and warmth in all directions, feel and sense the electromagnetic energy radiating from your physical heart to every cell and organ of your physical body and beyond. Notice what happens to you when you are in the midst of this heart-generated energy field.*

⁜ *Put in writing the effects and benefits you experience being under the influence of your very own heart-generated energy field.*

# Cherished Moments

*"I was seeing in a sacred manner the shape of all things in the Spirit.
And I saw that it was holy."*

—Black Elk—

Consider what you cherish. Ultimately, these are expressions such as love, caring, inspiration, respect, passion, and beauty. These soulful moments last and stand as the true eternal mark of a life well-lived. The sands of time generally sweep the rest away.

※ *Let your brain/mind drop into your heartspace. Sense everything softening within and around you.*

※ *In this gentle state, ask yourself, "What do I truly cherish?" Stay with this question for several minutes and make a conscious note of what comes to you. Write it down.*

※ *Mold a grateful heart of cherished moments, moments which mean the most to you. When you choose to let this be your habit, you become a living mandala of blessing and healing for your loved ones and community. Be the example.*

PRACTICE #78

# Free Your Imprisoned Splendor

*"The best introduction to astronomy is to think of the nightly heavens as a little lot of stars belonging to one's own homestead."*
—George Eliot—

Begin this day by acknowledging that you are the universe in miniature. In spiritual terms, the invisible dynamic energy of this infinite universe or Spirit is embodied as you.

Often, this truth feels inaccessible. My invitation to you today is to live in the heartfulness of poet Robert Browning's reminder to release your "imprisoned splendor" into expression.

Here's an intentional practice designed to create this release:

* *Sit, center in your heart and become still, breathing slowly and deeply. Feel the expansion of energy emanating from your heart.*

* *If it is daytime, breathe and expand your Spirit into the vast open space between yourself and the horizon. It's as if your Spirit is a flow of invisible energy filling up this large space. You're taking on the expansive nature of the universe.*

* *If you're experiencing this at night, breathe and expand into the space between you and a distant star. As Spirit, you have no circumference.*

* *May this splendor be aroused in you now.*

# Amplified Field

*"Healing is not a science but the intuitive art of wooing nature."*
—W. H. Auden—

Past emotional and psychological imprints are <u>not</u> all powerful. Let me bring you back to something I wrote in a daily writing. "Remember that the heart is an expanded energy field connected to and extending out in a large torus-shaped circle around you...Your amplified deep resonance with this heartspace is a way to provide a healing, soothing balm."

  ❋  *Breathe into your heartspace until you feel centered and focused in the moment.*

  ❋  *Now, like the energetic surge of witnessing a rising sun, feel the amplitude and power of the heart's energy circulating around and through you like blood through your veins.*

  ❋  *Utilize this practice throughout your day, especially when a past imprint shows up.*

  ❋  *Notice what happens, and write down what you have learned this day about your emotional and energetic landscape.*

PRACTICE #80

# 360-Degree Inspiration

*"Oh give these clay feet wings to fly to touch the face of the stars.*
*Breathe life into this feeble heart."*

—Loreena McKennitt—

You likely are aware of the voices within you, which exist for the sole purpose of reigning you in. You feel stuck in an adolescent paradigm which gives too much power to controlling parental voices from your past.

Rarely do you have access to a 360-degree experience of who you are because your mountaintop doesn't feel accessible. You feel this drag against your ascendency into full expression. There are times when you need to return to your mountaintop to capture a truer, more expansive vision of yourself and your life.

* *Stand up. If you can't stand, it's ok.*

* *Wherever you are, close your eyes, feel your feet firmly planted, and bring your mental focus to your heart.*

* *Now, in your inner visual awareness, go to your favorite mountaintop or high spot wherever it may be, real or imagined. From this vantage point, centered in your heart, gradually turn 360 degrees, taking in the view in all directions.*

* *Then say and feel, "I can see a great distance in all directions. Nothing is in my way no matter which way I turn. I am now prepared and ready to contribute all my gifts and talents to my community and world."*

* *Breathing slowly in and through your heart, stay with this vision, this feeling, these words. Resonate with this inspiration for as long as you like.*

* *Write down your feelings and insights from your 360-degree view.*

*Ed Conrad*

# Open to Receive

*"I love you for putting your hand into my heaped up heart and...*
*drawing out into the light all the beautiful and radiant things that no one else has*
*looked quite far enough to find."*

—Roy Croft—

There is a quality of love and warmth you greatly cherish and admire which is beautifully expressed through someone else. It could be a revered teacher, lover, friend, or family member.

- *Reconnect in this moment with the appreciation you feel for this beloved individual.*

- *Visualize the two of you sitting together face-to-face. This cherished person looks directly into your eyes, gently takes your hand, and begins pouring out heartfelt warmth and encouragement to you.*

- *Like a young flower turning toward the warmth of the sun, open to receive this personal blessing into your whole being. It slowly fills you up to overflowing. You simply continue to receive for as long as you choose.*

- *Feel your gratitude in your whole being for this revered person.*

# Being Like Bamboo

*"The bamboo or willow survives by bending with the wind."*
—Bruce Lee—

There is a lifelong challenge for all of us: How do we feel difficult feelings and not close our hearts? It requires wisdom and practice.

The wisdom is carved from repeatedly experiencing the excruciating effects of a closed heart, not only yours but the hearts of others. You come to realize there is a far better way to live. This wisdom leads to choosing to live differently through consistent practice.

The following three-phase practice is opening and bending like a bamboo. The healing and uplifting benefits are endless. The secret to mastering this practice is progressively making the fundamental shift to being heart-centered, so that your reptilian and emotional brain responses are not as easily triggered.

> *Consciously keep your heartspace open no matter what comes at you. (This is assuming you aren't in any physical danger.) This is supported by your inspired commitment to turn vulnerability and fear into energy and power and to maintain direct access to your Spirit/Higher Power.*

> *Choose to stay present with what you feel rather than defensively shutting down or reacting to what you feel or projecting onto someone else. This is facilitated and improved through conscious, connected breathing into your heartspace.*

> *Consciously flow compassion, encouragement, and goodwill out into your world.*

PRACTICE #83

# Becoming Heart-Headed

*"Every moment of every day your heart is having a conversation with your brain."*
—Gregg Braden—

The ageless wisdom of many sacred traditions teaches that when your heart and head are in harmony you become the light of all-possibility in your life. The following process helps keep your lamp turned on.

* *As you enter into today, practice conscious breathing with your attention on your heart.*

* *While feeling a current of loving energy flowing back and forth from your brain to your heart in an endless loop, send this powerful prayerful message to your brain/mind. "Great Spirit, the coherence of my heart and mind is established now in every breath I take and every choice I make. All aspects of who I am are synchronized. Grounded in this energy, I open now to experience the abundance of life today."*

* *Repeat the words of this simple prayer and keep your attention on the flow of loving energy between your heart and mind throughout your day.*

* *Put in writing what you experience from this prayerful state of coherence today.*

PRACTICE #84

# Letting Go

*"When you realize there is nothing lacking, the whole world belongs to you."*

—Lao Tzu—

Do you find yourself at times tightly clinging to the people and things in your life? You are not alone. Fear of loss and cultural and family conditioning have likely lured you into believing that the people, places, beliefs, and things of this world determine your worth, identity, and security.

The mystic in you is always calling upon you to connect with your unchanging core. Feel your love and passion for the people, things, and core beliefs of your life which you value. Alongside this very human experience, remember that your worth, security, and true identity arise not from the things of this world but from the depth and manifestation of spirit you express and share. That's it.

- ❋ *Connect with your heartspace.*

- ❋ *Turn your attention to your strongest attachments in this world...the persons, places, animals, things, points of view, and beliefs. Your subconscious knows what they are. There's no need to consciously list them all.*

- ❋ *Call all these pieces and parts of your human experience into your silent heart. For a few minutes, hold them all in this silence. Feel sincere gratitude and love for all of these aspects of your life.*

- ❋ *Remember, like your own child or any creation of yours, all of these relationships, feelings, things, and beliefs come to you and move through you, but ultimately they don't belong to you nor are they the measure of your identity. In the depth of your heartspace acknowledge this.*

- ❋ *Open to being untethered from all attachments and any fear of loss. Feel all clinging cease even if only for a few moments. In this lightness of being is the fertile soil for new beginnings and freedom from fear of loss. Love is letting go of fear. Begin.*

*Ed Conrad*

*Journal about what you are learning about truly letting go.*

# Redeem the Value of Time

*"You have found a very good reason to stop consuming time
and start appreciating what time provides."*

—Ed Conrad, *Heart Power*—

The choice is yours to put both feet firmly in the present moment and set forth to gather bits and pieces of inspiration and redemption and eventually return them to the soil of your family and community.

Consider your days as opportunities to put to rest the gospel of consumption. Commerce is vital. Consumption is not. In fact, consumption as a value and practice tears at the heart of being human.

The one reality of everyday life that is being voraciously consumed by many of us is time. It's as if we're in a trance and running a race with no finish line.

* *Slow way down; your breathing, and mental and physical activity. Return to your connection with your heartspace.*

* *Acknowledge and honor the built-in divine design in your being which requires that you set down the tools of work and productivity at least one-seventh of your time.*

* *Move through time this day by attending to what would be most nourishing, beautiful, restful, and inspiring. This quality of attention on what is truly rejuvenating is what you require from time to time. There is no urgency, task, or compulsive activity controlling you.*

PRACTICE #86

# The Spirit of You

*"There's a place for us, a time and place for us."*
—Stephen Sondheim—

I call you back to the dream of you imagined in someone's heart long ago before you were born. The truth remains that you are a dream come true.

When you look at the almost infinite forms of life that manifest in this multiverse, the reality that you have come and are having this human experience is against all odds. Welcome...

　❋　*Connect in your heart with the truth that all life is precious. Bring this awareness home and take it in that you are precious and extremely rare.*

　❋　*What is powerful spiritual medicine for you and quickly reconnects you to the essence of you? Serve it up for you today; your favorite song, poem, sacred verse, memory, or reading.*

　❋　*Say a prayer of thanks for the turning of the hoop of life which has created and brought you here as well as those you love.*

　❋　*Write your prayer of thanks, if you choose.*

PRACTICE #87

# Judgment-Free Awareness

*"Deep in my heart, I do believe, we shall overcome some day."*
—Pete Seeger—

Be aware of the ways you may be swiftly judging another. Is it based on a past event or their appearance, skin color, lifestyle, or political viewpoint? Remember how it feels when the tables are turned and critical judgment is directed at you. In either situation, you are diminished as well as the other.

* *Breathe into and get centered in your heartspace.*

* *Recall a time when you felt the sting of critical judgment directed at you from someone else. How were you affected? What did you feel? What did you actually want to receive from those who judged or turned against you? Make note of what that is.*

* *Connect to your core healing presence which is judgment-free.*

* *While centered in your judgment-free awareness, ask that love and compassion heal any tendency toward cruelty and judgment which have arisen from old fears. Treat others as you would want them to treat you. This is your mantra for today and always.*

*Ed Conrad*

# God-in-Training

*"You are the light of the world."*
—Jesus of Nazareth—

Ageless wisdom along with discoveries in physics and technology are revealing that you are particles and waves of light and energy specifically designed to manifest infinite possibilities. What was previously considered the realm of gods has now become a revelation of who and what you are.

You are here to love with all your heart, soul, mind, and strength. Stated more dynamically, you are a god-in-training in human form. You live to break the chains of long-standing assumptions which have hidden the truth of who you really are.

Being a divine-human is what you are here to learn to do well.

* *You can practice this moving meditation while walking, jogging, or on a treadmill or other exercise machine.*

* *Let your mantra be, "I am the light of the world, a god-in-training." Repeat this mantra while remaining centered in your heartspace.*

* *Imagine light pouring into you through the top of your head. Feel all heaviness flowing out of you into the earth.*

* *Imagine and feel yourself radiating and being the clearest truth of who you have come here to be.*

# Why Have You Come?

*"The powerful play goes on, and you may contribute a verse."*
—Walt Whitman—

What is your verse? What is your primary reason for being born into this world? There is a destiny, a singular inspiration that lives within you and only you. It's as if you've been summoned to give a gift and leave a legacy which contributes something precious to the heart of your community and our world. It's never too late.

✳ *Return to your center through heart-connected breathing. With your inner voice ask this question: "Why have I come to earth?"*

✳ *Hold this question in your heart throughout your day. Write down what comes to you. Open to the insight and direction it provides.*

PRACTICE #90

# The Power of One

*"I have been deeply influenced by the emerging story of how we all got here...those stars, pregnant with the elements that would eventually become you and me."*

—Dennis Rivers, *The View from the Milky Way—*

Doing the following simple practice with another restores sacred connection and awakens in both of you the strength and healing power of One.

- *Set aside time to completely be with another.*

- *Once you're together, breathe deeply, drop into your heart, and ask the one you're with to do the same.*

- *From this silent, amplified heartspace, open to experience a clear connection with your Divine Source and each other. There is no agenda, no have to's, nothing rote, no hyperactive impulse to impress or control what happens. Stay with this silent fusion of energy.*

- *Spend several minutes sharing what arises from this Oneness. Stay heart-connected while doing so.*

# Being Here Now

*"The miracle is to walk on the green Earth in the present moment, to appreciate the peace and beauty that are available now."*

—Thich Nhat Hanh—

Short memory clips of your life can make large imprints on your mental and emotional landscape. At any time, you can come under the influence of one of these clips via a conscious memory or an unconsciously triggered emotional or visceral experience.

Under these common scenarios, your everyday present moments can easily become a remake of your past. That's one way to live.

Consciously living in the present moment occurs because you honor the precious nature of the present moment. As Eckhart Tolle says, "Realize deeply that the present moment is all you have. Make the NOW the primary focus of your life."

Developing the capacity to remain heart-connected and present in the now is the way to unconditional happiness.

> ❋ *Invite all that you are into the present moment. Feel your heartbeat and slow your breathing. Close your eyes, clasp your hands together, and become deeply quiet and still. Your awareness is singly focused on your heart.*

> ❋ *Sit for a several minutes simply placing all your conscious attention on your heart. If your attention wanders away from your heart and the present moment, simply bring your full attention back to your breath and heartspace. This simple awareness practice is a powerful predictor of happiness.*

PRACTICE #92

# The Heart Leads and The Mind Follows

*"Listen my children with the ear of your heart."*
—St. Benedict—

Science is confirming that the heart is much more than an electromechanical pump. It is becoming evident that the heart is a powerful generator of its own form of intelligence and measurable energy which supports higher brain and immune system function.

The heart also serves as an inner compass always searching for the ways and means to heal, unite, love, and transform. The brain/mind, when operating beyond the scope of its capabilities, can too easily generate fearful, judgmental, controlling, and reactive responses.

> *Today, after a few moments of feeling centered in your heart, decide that the voice inside your head is no longer orchestrating your life. Your brain can beautifully and automatically perform all of its natural functions. However, it is your presence centered in your heart that is far better equipped to inspire, create, face adversity, and direct your life and relationships from this moment on.*

> *Vigorously declare that this shift in your seat of power begins now. Relax into it. Give thanks.*

PRACTICE #93

# Love Your Body

*"Someone had taken God out of my body."*
—Gabrielle Roth—

I pose this question to you. What if you honored your body as the carrier of Spirit, a sacred temple of the Divine? Consider that the vibration of the transfiguring spirit of all life is designed to be manifest in your body.

※ *As you put your clothes on today, imagine them enveloping you in the transfiguring presence of love. Feel this same presence of love as you place your arms and hands firmly around you.*

※ *Before you head into your day, sit quietly for a few minutes. While breathing into your heart, allow your body and senses to be fully immersed in this love.*

※ *Then, as you move through your day, sense that your whole being is fully clothed in this invigorating, transfiguring love. Love your body.*

※ *Put in writing all the ways that you could love your body; your personal temple for Spirit to express.*

# Be the Heart of the World

*"May the Holy Spirit guide us as we seek to heal and to nurture the earth and all of its creatures, to live in the midst of creation, and to love one another as brothers and sisters with all life."*

—U.N. Environmental Sabbath—

The gospel of Jesus in one word is love, a love which has no limits. Don't hold back. Love with all your heart, mind, soul, and strength. Be the heart of the world, a love without end.

*Stop what you are doing and take several slow, deep breaths. Focus on the lower center of your chest continuing to breathe slowly and deeply.*

*Keeping that focus, gently lean back just a bit, and stretch your arms straight out from your side with your chest open wide. Notice how this feels.*

*Now, while holding this sacred pose, for as long as you choose, radiate love and compassion out to the world from your center, your sacred heart. Let this feeling run deep. Do this at least twice today.*

# Begin at the End

*"Empower me to be a bold participant,... and to find treasures of joy, of friendship, of peace hidden in the fields of the daily you give me to plow."*

—Ted Loder—

What would bring you joy and fulfillment? You likely know what it would be. Rather than waiting for those experiences to occur at some future time, begin at the end.

Today's simple magical practice is an energizing creative way to remake the present. Your future is the offspring of the life you are creating now.

⁂ *Clearly identify the three or four primary experiences or things you want in life. Spend some time arriving at your answers. Be specific. Write them down.*

⁂ *Then, centered in your heart, take at least five minutes to feel the expansion of joy and fulfillment in your body and energy system, as if you have already received what you truly want. See in your mind's eye the places, people, and creative activities you are engaged in.*

⁂ *Now, sincerely feel grateful that this fulfillment is real and complete. End this practice with these words from your heart, "This or something better. Thank you."*

PRACTICE #96

# Light Power

*"Good people, most royal greening verdancy, rooted in the sun,
you shine with radiant light. In this circle of earthly existence you shine so finely,
it surpasses understanding."*

—Hildegard of Bingen—

Light, the glow of the universe that manifests in spectacular varieties, flows in, through, and all around us. In his writings, Jacques Lusseyran, blinded at age 8, invites each of us to realize that the light we see with our visual perception is a mere facsimile of the true radiant luminosity of eternal light within us.

Light is in the center of our being and in all creation. We've only just begun to comprehend and benefit from the spiritual technology of light. So much remains unknown, a vast mystery. Yet, you and I, along with the great mystics and sages, continue to explore all aspects of this universal radiance.

*For a few minutes, cease all outer activity. Allow your attention to move from your head to your heart. Breathe slowly and deeply with each inhale and exhale.*

*Call upon this universal light radiating out from your heartspace to revitalize and shine brightly in you. Feel and sense its warmth and energy.*

*Now bring the awareness of someone you care about into this light-filled energy. Let there be light. Let there be light in both of you. Enjoy this experience for as long as you like.*

# Slow Down Healing Prayer

*"O Earth...draw me down into your well of rebirth, and let my wounds become fertile gardens and let me be, let me live again."*

—Alla Renée Bozarth—

There is a healing presence and power within and around you always. You feel it more consistently when you slow down, really slow down. The impulsive urge is off the accelerator. Your senses quiet and any tendency to strain or fearfully react is released.

* *For five minutes, take the inspired action today to slow way down and set all mental and physical busyness aside. Become very still within and without. Promise to return to these activities shortly.*

* *While in this state of stillness, speak from your heart the following prayer: "Holy Presence, cause the miraculous healing energy of the heart of my being to gracefully remove old walls of fear and free me to live in love-affirming ways."*

* *Repeat this stillness and prayer at least three times this day, each time truly feeling the prayer.*

# Habit-Forming Appreciation

*"If people behaved with kindness and generosity to their fellows,
they could save the world."*

—Karen Armstrong, *The Great Transformation*—

Feeling and expressing appreciation can become habit-forming. Its fertile nature undoes sterile habits of cynicism and apathy. As appreciation grows, kindness grows and vice-versa.

Both then flow steadily from you, even in your innermost thoughts, feelings, and imaginings. Your only inclination is to pay them forward to others. This becomes a value-added way to live.

*Sow powerful seeds of appreciation and kindness into the soil of your thoughts, feelings, and movements of the day. Sense and see them as twin angels called to transform all forms of cynicism and apathy in your life and the lives of others.*

*Watch how subtle transformations occur and how appreciation and kindness flow back to you to complete an invisible circle.*

# The Field Beyond

*"Out beyond ideas of wrongdoing and rightdoing is a field. I'll meet you there."*
—Jalaluddin Rumi—

Consider in your heart these words of wisdom from Rumi, the great Sufi mystic. His potent poetic vision reminds you that often there are unrealized inspirations readily available which are blocked by the judgmental landscape of your mind.

* *After reflecting on Rumi's teaching for several minutes, make note of a current relationship, creative project, or inner conflict in your life which is stuck in a holding pattern. Apply his inspiring words of wisdom and encouragement.*

* *Relax and become still. Visualize and feel your mind dropping into your heart. From this coherent and more expansive state of heart and mind, ask that new wisdom make itself known to you and open you to new inspiration. Meet yourself there.*

* *Put the inspirations that emerge in writing.*

# About the Author

Ed Conrad, spiritual teacher, minister, and elder leader, is the founder/creator of The HeartWisdom Center in Eugene, Oregon, as well as the author of the acclaimed daily reader, *Heart Power, Going Deeper Into the Heart of Who You Are One Day at a Time* (revised version available June, 2018.)

Ed also served as the spiritual leader in Unity spiritual communities across the country for more than twenty-five years and is the founding minister of Columbine Spiritual Center in Boulder, Colorado and Unity in the Heart in St. Paul, Minnesota.

To contact Ed and find out more about The Heart-Powered Path, The Heart-Wisdom Center and related teachings, seminars, video podcasts, and audio heart-powered meditations or to schedule Ed as a guest speaker for your organization or spiritual community, or to schedule a private Heart-Powered Integration Session, go to https://www.heartpoweredpath.com.

Ed resides in Eugene, Oregon and frequents the rivers, forests, and Pacific ocean nearby and cherishes his two children, Hillary and Zachary, his five grandchildren, Elise, Pailey, Corah, Tanna, and Max and his beloved Candyce.

Made in the USA
Columbia, SC
03 March 2021